Priests in Secular Work

Participating in the Missio Dei

— JENNY GAGE —

Sacristy
Press

Sacristy Press
PO Box 612, Durham, DH1 9HT

www.sacristy.co.uk

First published in 2021 by Sacristy Press, Durham

Copyright © Jenny Gage 2021
The moral rights of the author have been asserted

All rights reserved, no part of this publication may be reproduced or transmitted in any form or by any means, electronic, mechanical photocopying, documentary, film or in any other format without prior written permission of the publisher.

Scripture quotations, unless otherwise stated, are from the New Revised Standard Version Bible: Anglicized Edition, copyright © 1989, 1995 National Council of the Churches of Christ in the United States of America. Used by permission. All rights reserved worldwide.

Every reasonable effort has been made to trace the copyright holders of material reproduced in this book, but if any have been inadvertently overlooked the publisher would be glad to hear from them.

Sacristy Limited, registered in England & Wales, number 7565667

British Library Cataloguing-in-Publication Data
A catalogue record for the book is available from the British Library

ISBN 978-1-78959-142-2

Contents

Acknowledgements iv

Introduction 1
Chapter 1. Growing into my vocation as a priest in secular work 4

Part 1: The Context 31
Chapter 2. Theological context: Between Pentecost and the Parousia 33
Chapter 3. How did we get here? A brief history 46
Chapter 4. Models of priesthood 51
Chapter 5. What do we mean when we talk about "having a vocation"? 58
Chapter 6. The research project 63

Part 2: The PSW 75
Chapter 7. Four PSW narratives 84
Chapter 8. Who are you? 105
Chapter 9. What do you seek? 126
Chapter 10. Where are you staying? 151

Postscript 172
Bibliography 177
Notes 187

Acknowledgements

When I embarked on a professional doctorate in 2012 on what it means to be a priest in secular work (PSW), it was with the intention of writing a book which would provide a theological underpinning for the PSW as a unique and distinct vocation. This emerged from my own experience, but it would have been of limited interest if it had only been about me. I therefore want to record the great debt I owe to the many PSWs who gave so generously of their time and experience both during my doctoral research (2012–19), and subsequently as I sought to update my research and to fill in some of the gaps. I am particularly grateful to the three other members of my co-operative inquiry group and the six people who agreed to be interviewed in depth.

I do not name these people because when I did my research, I gave an undertaking that I would do all I could to preserve the anonymity of participants. I hope that this will also enable other PSWs to locate themselves in the stories and quotations, however.

Two people I do want to name are Canon Ruth Goatly and Prebendary John Lees. Ruth and I supported each other through our professional doctorates, forging a deep friendship in the process. When John wrote his book *Self-Supporting Ministry: A Practical Guide*, I acted as a critical reader for him—he has now returned the compliment, providing an invaluable critique of my draft manuscript.

I would also like to acknowledge the help and support of my doctoral supervisors: Dr Zoë Bennett, the Revd Dr Ian McIntosh, the Revd Dr Michael Fass and the Revd Dr Andrew Stobart.

Finally, thanks to my husband, Andrew, who in addition to proof-reading, is unquestioningly supportive of my projects and enthusiasms.

Introduction

Will you then, in the strength of the Holy Spirit, continually stir up the gift of God that is in you, to grow in holiness and grace?
Ordination of Deacons[1]

Will you, then, in the strength of the Holy Spirit, continually stir up the gift of God that is in you, to make Christ known among all whom you serve?
Ordination of Priests[2]

In February 2020, I saw a letter in the *Church Times* from an ordinand, in which he stated that he had recently been told by "a senior clergyman that there was 'no theological model'" for worker priest ministry. I responded to say that there is, and that I was in the process of writing a book about just that. It is my hope that this book will show that there is indeed a theological model for a person who is a worker priest, minister in secular employment (MSE), priest in secular work (PSW), or any other name that such a person might choose to call themselves.

When my letter was printed three weeks later, I received a number of letters, mainly from people telling me about their experience of the discernment of their vocation as a worker priest or MSE. In addition, I received a letter from a long-standing Licensed Lay Minister (LLM).[3] She told me about the ministry she had exercised in her place of work, on a par with that of her ordained colleague, and asked:

> ... why it is thought that in situations where there is no sacramental ministry involved, a person can fulfil their calling as a Christian nurse, doctor, teacher, engineer, shopworker, whatever, better by being ordained priest?

The lay minister further said that she hoped that this book will contain:

> ... a chapter looking at the question of why the call to serve Christ in the world requires the person to be set apart by all the trappings of priesthood—any more than the call to preach and teach as a lay Christian requires it.

I want to be very clear that nothing I write in this book is in any way meant to say that I think ordained ministry is in some way better or more important than lay ministry, however recognized. In the workplace there is little obvious difference between lay and ordained, unless the ordained person wears a collar, and many (most?) do not. I do not want to set up unnecessary oppositions between lay and ordained, or between self-supporting and stipendiary ministry, or between full- and part-time ministry, or any other supposedly binary choice. For one thing, these are frequently not as binary as they initially appear; for another, these are not what is really important. What is really important is that we recognize that all of us have a vocation, a call from God, to be ourselves, whatever that might look like, and whatever form of ministry that might entail. One of the people I interviewed in my research told me of a time when, as a newish MSE, he was asked by a stipendiary colleague why he needed to be ordained. His response was that he did not need to be ordained, but that he was, and why did the colleague feel that this was an important question? Another of my interviewees, when I asked her why she had felt called to ordained ministry when it was going to make no difference at all to what she did at work, said that ultimately it was about God. It was God who called her to ordained ministry, and she was simply following that call.

Some of us are called to be priests and to work in parish ministry; some of us are called to be priests and work in secular employment; and some of us are called to lay ministry, in parish and/or in secular employment. In the end, as my interviewees recognized, it is about the call of God to each of us. That said, I believe there is a specific vocation to be a priest in secular work, and the purpose of this book is to describe it as a valid, theologically grounded model of ministry, important not only for those of us who recognize this as our vocation, but for the benefit of the church generally. As Ephesians 4:4–7, 11–12 puts it:

> There is one body and one Spirit, just as you were called to the one hope of your calling, one Lord, one faith, one baptism, one God and Father of all, who is above all and through all and in all.
>
> But each of us was given grace according to the measure of Christ's gift.
>
> The gifts he gave were that some would be apostles, some prophets, some evangelists, some pastors and teachers, to equip the saints for the work of ministry, for building up the body of Christ . . .

CHAPTER 1

Growing into my vocation as a priest in secular work

Jesus said: "You did not choose me, but I chose you."
John 15:16

There can be no purely objective account of what it means to be a priest in secular work. We all have biases, some recognized, some not. So that you can see some at least of mine, I start this book with an account of how I came to realize that the particular vocation to which God has called me is that of priest in secular work.

A brief note on terminology: my preferred name for myself and people like me is priest in secular work (PSW), although worker priest and minister in secular employment (MSE) are better known. How I came to choose PSW, and what the different names signify, is an important theme in this book. A rose may smell as sweet by any other name, but names matter, as they are more than labels.

In quotations from my journal or from people I interviewed, I use the name I recorded at the time—these also include M/PSE (minister/priest in secular employment).

This is discussed further in Chapter 5.

In 2005, when I first started to think that God might be calling me to ordained ministry in the Church of England, I started to keep a journal. Initially it was a way to process these unasked for and terrifying thoughts as I grappled with the enormity of such an idea. In due course, it helped me to unpack what I wanted to be able to articulate to diocesan vocations advisers and others. Over time, it developed into a spiritual journal, in which I charted my conversations with God as I reflected on what was happening in my life, and tried to work out answers to questions which drove me forward in discerning the shape of my vocation. Quotations in this chapter are from the journals which I have kept ever since with varying levels of diligence. Reading through these journals, as I started to prepare this chapter, has reminded me that the relatively calm place in which I find myself now has been hard won, and that the account of my sense of vocation I can now articulate has emerged through much questioning about my sense of who I am, about God's will and my place in God's economy.

A personal piece of research often starts as a way of scratching an itch. My journals contain a detailed account of the itch that became increasingly insistent, leading me into a lengthy research project. I was driven by questions such as "who am I now?" and "what am I for now?"—"now" meaning now that I was an ordained priest in the Church of England, but while I was still working in the particular secular employment which paid me, and in which I spent most of my working hours. A sense of uncertainty about my identity ("who am I now?") and my purpose ("what am I for now?") started as soon as I was ordained deacon. One Thursday to Saturday at the end of June 2009, I was on retreat with other ordinands, nervous and excited. On the Saturday, the ordaining bishop laid hands on me, saying, "Send down the Holy Spirit on your servant, Jenny, for the office and work of a deacon in your Church."[4] On the Sunday, I attended three services, wearing an unaccustomed clerical collar, and "read myself in" at one of them—meaning I read the terms of my licence to the congregation. On the Monday, I accompanied my incumbent in various parish duties. On the Tuesday, I went back to my secular job and carried on as if nothing had changed—which in many ways it had not. The following year, I did it all again when I was ordained priest, except that I presided at the Eucharist for the first time rather than reading myself in.

Initially my focus was on getting to know people, preaching far more often than I had as an ordinand, and assisting four priests in five different churches,[5] which was quite a learning curve. I became aware that gradually my sense of my self was also changing, however: the itch

I felt an urge to scratch was my need to make sense of the ontological change which was an inevitable consequence of all that had changed and continued to change in my life.

Although I wondered if starting a research project "would be self-indulgent, taking me away from active ministry to enjoy study, research and writing", and so might be considered a form of navel gazing, in early 2012, I went ahead with an application to join a professional doctorate programme, recording that:

> I have been called to hold together the tensions of the MSE form of priesthood, to reflect on them, to develop my own self-understanding of what this might mean—and . . . to disseminate and make public what I find out. What a calling!

I had come to feel that it was a part of my vocation that I should do a research project on what it means to be a priest in secular work in order that I could write a theological rationale for this model of priestly ministry, claiming it as part of God's providence. At times, however, I had to struggle with doubts that I would finish, or that if I did, whether it would be of any use other than my own personal satisfaction. In Lent 2016, I wrote:

> I've done my Lent reading in bursts, rather than daily. One that really struck me was in *Taunts*[6] for day 7—"You are so naïve". This came only a few days after a diocesan ministry team meeting where I felt that all I am trying to do on behalf of Self-supporting Ministers (SSMs),[7] and especially M/PSEs (Minister/Priests in Secular Employment), won't even create a ripple—that the juggernaut of the church will continue, crushing those like me who have the temerity to think they might change things. But the response to the taunt is "allow your reasons for hope to rise once more to the surface". And so I must continue, trusting God to walk with me, and hold me when necessary.

That walk with God has continued, and in this book is the story of my growth into the vocation which I feel called to live and to describe for the benefit of you, my readers, and of the church of which I am a part.

A brief biography

I had first recognized a vocation to ordained ministry soon after leaving university, when I was in my early twenties. As a child, I attended the local Baptist church with my family, and was baptized there shortly before my fifteenth birthday by full immersion in water. In 1969, I left home for university determined to be the next Marie Curie, but by the end of the first year, I had realized that science and I were not well suited to each other. During my fourth term, therefore I changed to study theology. Prior to leaving home, I had rejected the faith of my childhood and teenage years, and started my theological studies as a person of no particular faith. I found God—or perhaps God found me—as I read Genesis with a commentary by Gerhard von Rad.[8] I found my way back into the Baptist church in my university city, in due course taking on leading the youth group, and after graduation becoming a lay preacher for Baptist churches in local villages.

Believing that God was calling me to ordained ministry, I went through the discernment process of the Baptist Union, and I entered a Baptist theological college in October 1974. The first two terms were wonderful: I thoroughly enjoyed the opportunity to take up theology again, feeling that this time around I could do so much better than I had previously with my late start on the course. I also enjoyed the experience of a student pastorate in a nearby village in the third term under the supervision of an experienced minister in the nearby town.

Things started to go wrong when he became seriously ill, and was hospitalized for a time, and, coincidentally, I was beginning to unravel, gradually becoming more and more dissociated from the people around me. I was diagnosed with depression and spent several weeks as a day patient in a psychiatric ward. I was still trying to study, but the day that I submitted an essay which my tutor told me was not even O-level standard was the day that I gave up on that. Writing it had been so hard, physically as well as mentally, as I struggled to grasp my pen and to form letters and words in ink, never mind coherent sentences. In the end, I asked for a year's leave of absence, an offer which was accepted with gratitude by the college staff, who were struggling to know what to do with me. In the summer of 1975, I started work as a secretary, and got on with life. As time passed, I knew that I was not going back, that that phase of my life was over.

Or so I thought, for it seemed that God had other ideas. In 2001, we moved to the cathedral city in which we now live. My husband, who is an ex-cathedral chorister, went to Evensong at weekends, and regularly asked me if I would like to go with him. To start with, I generally refused: I was writing up a PhD in maths education, while working full-time as a maths educator, and I needed all my weekends to wrestle with my data and my thesis. In time, however, I did start to go with him—and was awestruck by cathedral choral Evensong. It felt like being allowed to eavesdrop on the music of the angels. Over time, we started to go to the Sunday morning Eucharist and began to get involved in the life of the congregation.

I had left the Baptist church in my early thirties—by then I had four small children, and I found it hard to cope with wordy church services, and the expectation that of course I would want to help with children's work. Over the years that followed, I passed through Quaker meetings, and Methodist, United Reformed Church (URC) and Church of England churches, and eventually an ecumenical church, simply looking for somewhere that would welcome my children (not the quietest) and me, and not expect me to have anything to do with looking after children— that became even more important as a criterion for choosing a church once I became a teacher! At the ecumenical church, I became acquainted with a variety of styles of worship and liturgies. I was fairly dismissive of choral Evensong, however, regarding it as overly formal and difficult to get into, and frankly a bit elitist.

When I left the Baptist college, I became first a secretary and then a PA (read glorified secretary). I had learnt to type and do shorthand prior to going to the college, because it seemed a useful thing to do if I wanted to earn money while I went through the discernment process and during vacations. What I really wanted, once the idea of ordained ministry went away, however, was to have children—and I did, four of them in just over five years. I became a stay-at-home mum, encouraged by my own mother not to think about working at least until they were at school. I coped with the boredom and lack of intellectual stimulation by starting a degree with the Open University at about the same time that I became pregnant for the third time. I chose to study maths because I had enjoyed it at school, and I knew I would not have time to do the reading and thinking that writing essays would require. Whenever the children were asleep or in someone else's care, I studied, falling in love with maths all over again.

I carried on with my studies when my then husband's job took us to the USA in the autumn of 1982, initially for two to three months, and then for a further period of three months. Starting up a new life in Arizona, with four small children, was a challenge, but one that I was happy to take on. We became part of a church community, who played a large part in helping me to flourish. I became aware that many of the mothers were working, and expected to do so, and that, combined with forming a new life for myself and my children from scratch, gave me a sense of my own potential that I had lost.

We returned to the UK in the spring of 1983, and my life changed dramatically in the years that followed. In 1984, we moved house to a remote farmhouse in the Peak District, and in 1985 I ended the marriage I had entered into as an undergraduate in 1971. Needing to earn a living, I brought my Open University studies to an end, as by then I had done enough to get a degree, and did a PGCE in maths. In the autumn of 1986, I became a secondary school maths teacher.

The stress of the breakup, being on my own with four still quite young children, moving house twice, and starting teaching, not to mention driving daily round trips of between forty and seventy miles during my PGCE year,[9] took its toll, however, and my mental state gradually went downhill. I just about survived my probationary teaching year, but in my second year I was ill enough to be first a day patient, and then an in-patient, at a nearby psychiatric hospital. While still a day patient, I had reached a point where I phoned the minister of the church we were then attending to say that I could cope no longer, and would he please arrange for my children to be taken into care. I am so thankful that he did not do that, but instead got hold of my parents, from whom I had been hiding, ashamed of the depths I had reached. Recovery was slow, with family and friends hugely important.

Just after Christmas 1989, we moved to Milton Keynes, where I started a new job, keen to put the past behind me. There I was able to rebuild my confidence and my life, continuing to find help and support through being part of a church community, but also developing my teaching skills. From the summer of 1988 onwards, I was involved again with the Open University, initially doing a week's stint as a summer school tutor on the maths foundation course, and over time becoming a part-time tutor-counsellor, with a new group of students to teach every February to October, as well as summer school work on a number of different courses. I also helped school students as a private tutor, work I really enjoyed, particularly identifying the specific blocks to understanding that were holding them back.

By 1998, I had been accepted as a part-time doctoral student at the Open University, working towards a PhD which examined aspects of my professional practice, so when early in the autumn term of 2000 I saw an advert for a job which would involve new ways of teaching as part of a University of Cambridge schools' outreach programme, I went for it. I started that job in January 2001, and we moved the following April to Ely where we still live. In 2009, I was ordained deacon at Ely Cathedral, and in 2010, I was ordained priest, while continuing my secular work.

At Easter 2013 I took early retirement, but continued to work on a book with a colleague, with whom I had been collaborating previously, and to do teacher professional development workshops around the UK. I also continued to go out to South Africa, where I had been involved in a maths education institution since January 2006. I enjoyed these aspects of my work and was happy to continue them, keen to remain a priest in secular work. When eventually my teaching dried up, because I was no longer doing anything which would have brought work in, I was heavily involved in my research on PSWs. I felt that, although this was church-based, the actual work of research and writing was sufficiently similar to much of what I had done previously in my secular work to count as keeping my PSW status alive.

The questions which drove my research

Who am I?
When I simultaneously looked forward to, and feared, and then coped with, the birth of my first child in late 1976, I did not have the language or concept of ontological change. In retrospect, however, I see many parallels between what happened to me then, and what happened to me as a result of my ordinations in 2009 and 2010. In both cases, I knew in the abstract that I would be changed by my new status, but I had no way of anticipating what those changes would feel like. Although there was a clear continuity between who I was beforehand and who I was afterwards, there was also a sense in which there was a break in my identity—a specific day and event when everything changed, and I was no longer the same person.

There were many other parallels. As a new mother, I did not have much time to think about how my identity was changing, but as I learnt how to care for my child—the doing of being a mother—I also grew into being "mummy", so that this designation stopped feeling like a set of clothes bought for someone else that I was simply trying on for size, and became comfortable, and, over time, part of my skin. As a new deacon, and then priest, as I learnt how to do things, over time I began to feel more comfortable in my collar and cassock, so that I no longer felt as if I were acting a part. In the early days, weeks and months following my ordination as a deacon, I felt I no longer quite fit into my skin, that I needed to work out who I was all over again, and to get used to being that person, in the same way that I had had to get used to being "mummy" to my child. With my children, I am just "mum" now, and it feels entirely natural, totally taken for granted. Similarly, I became used to being "Reverend Jenny", although wearing my collar and robes is still something I think about—when I wear them, when I do not, and why.

Reading books that I hoped would provide some answers and advice was not always as helpful as it might have been, on one occasion recording in my journal:

> It's all very well to talk about deacons being bridges between church and world, being liminal people—but what does that

actually mean in practice? Talking theoretically, without case studies or examples, just made me feel inadequate, unprepared and bewildered. As C [a fellow new deacon with whom I had trained, also in secular work] said in an email . . . yesterday he was on placement at the airport; today he's a . . . geologist—so who is he? And for me, yesterday, I was a curate, today I'm a maths educator—so who am I?

In another journal entry a few days later, I described a conversation with someone else from my training course, in which I had talked about the difficulty I was finding in moving from Monday (spent in the parishes) to Tuesday (back in my secular job), and my lack of any clear sense about what it meant to be a deacon when I was in my workplace. A subsequent entry read:

This is a gift. It comes at a price. (Florence and the Machine[10].)
Who do people say that I am?

I had looked forward to ordination throughout my training course and placements. Once it had happened, I found myself needing to work out who I was all over again, feeling that although God had entrusted me with a very precious gift, that gift was costly, and the cost was my sense of my own identity. A few months later, I was at a deacons' training session on preparing to celebrate the Eucharist. I found standing behind the altar, speaking the words of the *Sursum Corda*, scary, strange and awe-ful. I was overtaken by a sense of ontological change taking place, and awed by the thought that soon I would be a priest, part of Christ's priesthood, for the rest of my life.

I reflected on what one book I was reading called the masks that we wear—wife, daughter, mother, friend—that they are so much more than masks because they are part of our selves, realizing that that is why it took me time to get used to being a deacon, because that too needed to become part of me. Being ordained priest would, I mused, be so much more, as fundamental to my sense of my self as daughter, wife, mother—all non-negotiable, never to be undone. I could undo being married to a particular person, perhaps, as indeed I had done earlier in my life, but I could not undo having been a wife, any more than I could undo being a daughter and a mother, whatever might happen to my parents or my children. I thought that being a priest would be:

> Part of the essence of me, more so than teacher which... but no. I was going to say that could be given up. But of course there's a difference between being a teacher and being paid to be a teacher! I am daughter, wife, mother, teacher, deacon and soon I shall add priest to that list. All are so much part of me that I cannot conceive of myself without them. Whoever emerges, as new life breaks open the old self, will still be all of those.

What am I for?

The question "what am I for?" resonated throughout my journals from my ordination as a deacon onwards. It formed a subtext to many conversations with other members of the ministry team I joined at that point, and also to discussions with colleagues in my secular job. It became particularly relevant in my secular employment when, from about 2009 onwards, our funding issues became even more acute than normal, and there were times when I was not at all sure that I would still have a job in six months' time or at the end of the year. The question "what am I for?" was generally triggered by the prospect of change of some kind, which made me consider all over again the nature and context of my vocation—did I want to be a (non-stipendiary) parish priest, for instance? Was it time to leave maths education? What about going back to South Africa for longer?

Once I had started the PGCE course which qualified me to teach in British schools in 1985–6, it had never occurred to me that I might one day cease to be a teacher, other than retiring when the time came. Even when I moved out of direct classroom teaching to work in a schools' outreach project, I still thought of myself as a teacher, albeit not based in a school any more. As soon as I entertained the prospect of ordination, that simple equation of identity = teacher changed, and with it my sense of knowing what my basic purpose was (I took my family commitment as a fundamental given).

The question "what am I for?" was a kind of shorthand for questions to do with priority—did becoming a deacon and then priest take priority in some way over being a teacher, or not? When I had to decide how to prioritize my time and energies, which would take precedence? Was I a teacher who happened to spend Sundays dressed up in robes and flying around the countryside from one village church to another? Or was I a priest who happened to earn their living through teaching? Every time I decided to make my life a bit simpler and less fraught by minimizing one aspect of what I did, something would emerge which would so appeal to me that there could be no question of giving up either teaching or ministry, or even doing less of either.

In 2011, I started thinking about further academic work, given that my MA dissertation had been deemed excellent by the three people who had read it (my supervisor and the two people marking it). A meeting with the diocesan Director of Ministry was on the horizon, to discuss the direction of my ministry through the rest of my curacy and beyond, but I realized that first I needed to work out what my "non-negotiables" were. One was being involved in public worship, which I saw as "fundamental to who I am now", but I also found myself reading online prospectuses for DMin courses, and enquiring:

> . . . about the suitability of a research area on ministers in secular employment. Am I in the throes of a life choice? The stuff about "what next" has crystallized into the question "what am I for?"—meaning what does God want me to be.
>
> The question for me at the moment is whether ministry through study, writing and perhaps some teaching, in addition to what I'm doing at [my secular workplace] is enough. Writing that I think—how absurd! What does "enough" mean in this context? Why do I feel that I have to be visibly doing obviously ministerial things?

Reflecting on it all, while at a Benedictine monastery that I visited from time to time between 2009 and 2012, the virtue of stability, of staying put, was at the fore: "being content to be who I am now, being content and fulfilled in the present moment, not mentally rushing ahead all the time". What finally emerged from all this was that I would continue my curacy, that I would start a professional doctorate in September 2012, and, from the beginning of October, would drop my secular employment to three days a week. That sounds as if I had settled something, but not much later I was speculating about the possibility of going out to South Africa for an extended working visit!

From 2010, the videoconferencing teaching that I had been doing had been phased out. Initially we focused on producing videos of experts explaining aspects of their field for schools, with accompanying resources, but as funding for those projects ran out, I started doing more work preparing resources for our schools' website. Where I had worked mainly with one colleague, whose expertise was in the technical aspects of videoconferencing and video production, the new team which I joined during 2011 consisted of some ten people, mainly teachers, but also two IT experts. Funding, and the need to seek it and to satisfy funders, prevented overall direction in terms of educational benefit. Although some of the team were adept at making the requirements of funders fit their agendas, I struggled with what appeared to me to be a lack of strategic direction, and to find my own role in the team.

During the summer of 2011, issues between members of the team came to a head with a meeting which I described as "dreadful", despite the fact that I felt "I was the initiator". I called attention to the fact that our team leader was emailing about something else during the meeting, and then made a remark about her absence from a particular event, thus creating an opportunity for "an onslaught" from two other people. After the meeting, she called me into her office, where she "accused me of being vindictive, and said she thought my inter-personal skills were better than that". I apologized, but "was left feeling hurt, and anxious that I'd acted badly not only as a human being but also as a priest". When I emailed her later in the day, she responded that she had moved on, leaving me unsure what it might all mean for our relationship, and with many questions about what it meant for me to be a priest in my workplace.

While all this was going on, there were family issues also: my father was in hospital in Norwich for a prolonged period, and my youngest daughter was suddenly taken into hospital in London with a recurrence of the glandular fever that she had suffered in her late teens. I was finding life hard going, especially at work:

> Overall, I just want to run away from the [professional development] day, and to rapidly drop the number of things for which I'm responsible. I'm really struggling.

I was signed off work (both my secular employment and my curacy) for a fortnight on the grounds of stress. I had decided that when the projects I was involved with in my secular work were finished, I was going to retire, which would probably be the following spring. I had a long conversation with our full-time stipendiary team vicar (not my training incumbent), in which:

> I identified issues about being in a liminal place—between middle-aged worker and young retired. I'm losing my identity as an educator, as I plan for retirement and perhaps self-employed status next spring. And this all raises the question of who I am. Mother, wife, priest . . . anything else? Is that okay? And what does my priesthood look like as time passes?

By the summer of 2012, when the team vicar announced she was leaving to become the incumbent of a group of churches in another diocese, I found myself in discussions with the archdeacon and rector about taking on her role, possibly as a house-for-duty associate priest. The house-for-duty bit was not going to work, because my husband needed easy access to the railway station, which would not have been the case in the village with the available house, but the role was certainly a possibility. As I thought about it, mentally thinking myself into that space, I was not at all sure that it was a good fit despite the ongoing problems in my secular workplace.

I was also still struggling with working out what it meant to be a priest in my secular workplace:

> Sometimes I take myself too seriously as a priest at work, and try too hard to fit into what I see as a priestly role. I think it works

best when I forget about it consciously, and just let God work through me—when I don't get in his way. Yesterday, I think I got in the way.

In July 2012, at an international maths education conference in Seoul, I had been troubled by various ailments, which I struggled to communicate effectively to the Korean pharmacist I went to for help. Returning home, my GP told me I had shingles, and I was signed off work for a fortnight. Soon after that, I took a few days' leave to go on retreat: "I feel I'm at a crossroads, and the seeds of the new are already forming . . . ". I spent quite a bit of time outside, focusing on the detail of a single flower, and trying to persuade myself that I did not need to be "for" anything, that just as a flower is perfect in itself, so too am I: "It doesn't have to justify itself in any other way, it simply is what it is."

Returning home, I confirmed with myself yet again that "I'm sure that my vocation is not to be a full-time vicar, stipendiary or otherwise." Back at work, I talked to our Deputy Director about dropping from four days a week to three, so that in addition to a day other than Sunday for ministry, I would have a day for writing and for sabbath time, but my new line manager was not in favour.

What am I looking for?
Time passed. On retreat a year later, I noted that the feeling of being lost encapsulated in the question "what am I for?" had become joy, "sheer joy in being alive and being me". My retreat director pointed me towards John 1:37–39, suggesting I stay with the question "what are you looking for?" Quite a lot, it seems:

> The trouble is, I want it all—[benefice], Prof Doc, S[outh] A[frica] maths ed, not to mention family. Then there's the Prob book[11] . . . and the SA books[12] . . . How to hold it all together is the question, since the prospect of letting any of it go feels quite wrong.

Although I had retired from paid employment at Easter 2013, I continued to work with one of my former colleagues on our approach to teaching probability, and I continued to be involved in the South African teacher professional development work.

By the autumn of 2014, I had decided that the time had come to leave the benefice where I had served my title and then been licensed as a part-time SSM associate priest. There was an SSM curate in the deanery who was looking for a house-for-duty post, and the house that I had not wanted to live in was still available. She duly arrived, ready to become the SSM associate priest in the benefice at the end of her curacy, which freed me up to look around and see where I might be more needed.

I went on retreat for Holy Week in 2015, preparing myself for my licensing in the new group of parishes at a Road to Emmaus service on the afternoon of Easter Day. I had agreed to preach at the service, and was working on it while I was away, wanting it to be my "calling card", setting out the shape of the ministry I anticipated. As I wrote, and rewrote again and again, I decided to focus on a sentence of Jürgen Moltmann's: "God is our happiness; God is our torment; God is the wide space of our hope." I don't now know what books I took with me, so I can't trace this—I don't know if it is in a book I have by Moltmann, or whether I found it referenced by someone else, but I do know that it spoke to me then, and still does now. What I was looking for, I knew, was to serve God as a priest in both church-based ministry and through my secular work. I had ceased to be in directly paid employment, but I was still involved in maths education, and I knew that we were not yet done with each other. I still wanted it all, and to be able to express my priesthood in the different contexts in which I had a stake.

The unfolding of my vocation to be a PSW

In 2005, when I first started my spiritual journals, when the possibility of ordained ministry emerged again after so many decades since that first sense of call back in my early twenties, I wrote: "I don't have to do this. Yet I feel my own personal growth is tied up in it as well as the importance of meeting other people at a deeper level." At that early stage in the discernment process, I appreciated the affirmation of my call given to me by two experienced priests to whom I was talking; I was less happy that it appeared unlikely that I would be able to enter paid ministry, meaning I would need to continue to support myself financially in other ways. I wanted to throw myself into the process 100 per cent, but was discovering that this might not be possible, at least not in the only way I knew—that of being a full-time stipendiary priest.

Then in October 2005, I met an MSE, a breed of priest I had not previously realized existed. I had been sent to spend a busy Sunday in a nearby benefice, to discover what it was like, perhaps to be put off? I duly attended the 8 a.m., 9.30 a.m. and 11 a.m. services at the two churches in the benefice. The 9.30 a.m. was led by the MSE, who then preached at the 11 a.m. Travelling between the two in his car, I found out more about him and his sense of vocation.

And there it sat for quite some time. As will become clear in the pages of this book, many who self-identify as worker priests or MSEs received their calling through their secular work, or knew from the start that it would be a significant locus for their ministry. I did not. Indeed, I see from my journal that when, in December 2005, the Diocesan Vocations Adviser I was seeing at that point asked me what kind of a priest I thought I was called to be, there was no sense that my secular work might play any part in it.

When I went to my BAP[13] in February 2007, however, the group exercise I had prepared had evolved from thinking about theological and mathematical resonances in resources I was working on in my secular work. Later, in early November 2007, a few months after I had started the training course leading to ordination, I wrote in my journal that I was using my work as a maths educator as a context for my theological reflections, focusing on the maths of labyrinths and mazes, and the maths of churches, mosques, synagogues and temples. These were topics which featured in videoconferences and workshops I led with students and with teachers at the time, and both were a way of making connections between what I did in my daily, secular work and my theological studies. Writing about this now, I notice that the connections I was making were conceptual, bringing together theological and mathematical ways of thinking, not about how I might be a witness or pastoral support in my workplace.

Later that month, I recorded going to "a meeting of the MSE group". This group was started by the MSE I had met in 2005. I am not sure exactly when it started, but I do remember that I should have been going to a meeting on the evening of the day my BAP finished, and not making it because I was exhausted! The entry in November 2007 mentions the liminal nature of "NSM/MSE" (Non-stipendiary Ministry/Ministry in Secular Employment), and that it is perhaps not surprising that people therefore:

> ... feel some sense of hurt at not being included/remembered because we are not wholly in the ministerial camp. And conversely, perhaps we are often going to feel some sense of exclusion in our work-places (if people know that we are priests or intending to be) because of people's perceptions of what a priest is.
>
> This picks up things I've read about being on the margins, and the margins being where we should be, but also sometimes being uncomfortable places to be. Perhaps we are necessary reminders for people of a dimension they would prefer to ignore.

As far as I can see, this is the first point in my journals where it is clear that I am self-identifying as a PSW, and where I begin to reflect on the nature of that vocation. I continued by musing on how all that I had previously taken for granted—the "givens" of my life—was changing, not least my feelings about my secular job. A little later, I was writing:

> On Saturday, we had an MSE group meeting at ... Lots of useful discussion on how ministry and work are related, what the role of the priest in a secular environment is, etc. At our next meeting, I am to say something about how I see being a priest in [my secular context] ...

Before long, I was asking myself if I felt that being a priest would be the most important thing in my life. What about my husband, children, father? What about my secular job?

> I think all of them need to become part of my vocation so that there is no separation, no tension between being a priest on the one hand and other loyalties on the other.... Work and indeed all life can be sacramental, but this has to be thought through, not to be left as a fuzzy, romantic notion.... I need to reflect on them and on how they fit together, not just assume that getting on with things will cause integration to happen.

As I described above, there were periods throughout the years between ordination in 2009 and retiring from paid employment in 2013 when I thought about leaving my secular job, not because I no longer enjoyed it, but because I felt "pulled in a different direction". Looking back, I see a pattern: I would become restless, struggling with my questions about who I was and what I was for; I would ask God for clear direction; I would find answers in both parish ministry and in my secular work. I felt equally at home/not at home in both, absorbed by the work in both, but somehow not entirely integrated.

I made several attempts to reduce the tension I experienced in keeping both going. In December 2009, one of the tutors on my training course resigned to go abroad, and even though I had only left six months previously, I decided I was going to apply for the post. I decided that, in any case, the following summer would be the end of my involvement in maths education, observing that the "sense that it's time to move on is very strong". I realized that I was building "castles in the air", but that the urge to move on in some way was very real, and that I felt I had reached a fork in the road. In mid-January 2010, I was interviewed for the post, but did not get it: it did not help that the Principal told me it was very close.

I continued to "struggle with the whole work/ministry thing" during 2010, as the day of my priestly ordination drew ever closer. I felt that I was being stripped down, as I waited through the days. I was aware that I did not want to be a full-time curate; if that had once been my hope, it had evaporated. I also realized that I did not actually want to leave my secular workplace, because I was "still energized by the prospect of teaching maths and creating new resources"—although there was continuing uncertainty about funding for the project in which I was employed. I was also enjoying leading a hands-on maths club in which children from one of the schools in our parishes came into church to discover the maths around them there.

In one of the addresses at the ordination retreat, the speaker reminded us that:

> ... we are sheep struggling to be shepherds. We are not in a personal journey with God, to be lived in a holy ghetto, but we are in community, struggling to be shepherds to the people with whom we are placed.

That gave me a new insight on why I was still in my secular workplace. I thought about John 10:11–12, that "the hired hand ... sees the wolf coming and leaves the sheep and runs away ... ", and wondered if that was what I was trying to do.

Ongoing reading led me to a passage about St Benedict, and that for him "all work, whatever it might be, if done in love, was a sacrament".[14] Throughout those early years in ordained ministry, I continued to think about what I wanted to do, and what the nature of my vocation was. My training incumbent thought I would want to be full-time in parish ministry if I could—"well, actually, no", and through conversation with a fellow PSW about what it means to be such, I felt encouraged to stay in my secular work as long as possible. I recognized that "this period [was] the data on which any later thinking and writing I do will be based". And so it has proved to be! Living in the tension over a number of years gave me the experience needed to inform the development of my thoughts about what it all means.

Following my trip to South Korea, when I had returned home tired and exhausted, suffering with shingles, while I was still isolating myself from other people, I decided to go into one of our churches to pray:

> I felt a sense of God's loving care of me, I'm not sure how else to put it into words. The question that keeps coming to me is "I don't know what I'm for, what my purpose is." ...
>
> [I] wonder if there is a progression—I glory in my abilities and achievements, I want them to be recognized and used in the

church or in my ministry in some way, I fail to recognize that these are God-given and that they can be taken away. I now feel that I have less to offer, that I am moving away (or being moved away) from all the active stuff, so that I am forced into a position where all I can do is humbly wait on God, for there is nothing else left. I have no control over what happens to me, especially illness and the lack of energy I am currently experiencing. And I need to be patient and to listen.

I started trying to unpack my thinking about what it meant to me to be a priest while remaining in secular employment, writing in my journal:

> I talked with [my spiritual director] about the tension of being a bridge, crossing gaps, being at the edges to hold different environments together. She asked if it might be a vertical bridge as well as a horizontal one. And it comes to me that the bridge is Jesus, but the priestly task is to embody it in this point of time and space. Perhaps that encapsulates what I'm for, what my calling is as an MSE, the priestly nature I am being asked to take on.
>
> It seems my research is as much as anything about finding an identity, a name, which does not relate specifically to what I have been doing up to now, but which will be the lens through which this next part of my life is to be discerned.

But . . .

Being a public Christian in the workplace

A disagreement with a work colleague early in 2009 resulted in considerable heart-searching over what it meant to me to be not only a Christian in my workplace, but a Christian who would soon be ordained deacon. I was struggling to find a balance between wanting to accommodate what other people wanted or expected of me, and "becoming a shadow of myself, apologizing endlessly if I can't", and in the end not being authentically myself. A month later, however, I was writing in my journal about a conversation with a different colleague in which she had told me about mental health issues she was experiencing, and asked me to pray with her. Following my ordination, I found myself in discussions with my training incumbent and our team vicar, describing these and similar events, and reflecting on how I saw being a deacon in my place of work. A few weeks later, I read a letter from an MSE in the *Church Times*, in which the writer had said that you cannot be a part-time priest or a part-time human being. For me, that meant being a priest at work through presence, although I did not have a very clear idea at that point what I meant by that.

But maybe I knew more than I remember. On the pre-deaconing ordination retreat, the retreat leader suggested we ask for a particular grace from God. I had no idea what to ask for, until it came to me that I wanted "to be someone who can bring the peace of God's presence to others. To bring sabbath." In my pre-priesting journal, I was still engaging with the theme of sabbath, but also about the value of being able to laugh at myself when I was being too pretentious! Was it pretentious to speculate that "one person's silence and prayerfulness can influence others around them", and that this might be part of the gift of sabbath?

As I re-read my autumn 2010 entries, I was reminded of the three sessions on how our work contributes to our faith that I attempted to run in the faith space near to my workplace, which I had organized with the chaplain to staff. He came to the first two, one other person came to the second, and no one at all to the third. I still feel the embarrassment of that, and it demonstrated to me why workplace ministry is rarely about doing the kinds of things we might do in parish ministry. A lunchtime session, which would have required people to leave their workplace to go to a faith space ten minutes' walk away, was probably never going to get off the ground, given that most people spent their lunch-breaks either at their desks or relaxing in the communal meeting places nearest to hand. There are also issues about the kinds of activity that feel appropriate when one is in work mode.

Around that same time, I was also reminded that in a secular environment like a university, faith and faith spaces are not neutral. I had seen an advert asking for people willing to support others going through any kind of formal process involving accusations of bullying or harassment, and, as our project Director and Deputy Director were both very supportive, I had put myself forward. At interview, I was quite open about being a priest and that being my motivation for offering myself—I was not selected, despite being very well qualified for the role.[15]

There were opportunities to exercise a priestly ministry of sorts in the workplace. Since I had "outed" myself several people had talked to me about personal problems or about church-based issues. One colleague, for instance, came to see me to discuss the appropriateness, or otherwise, of her being a godmother to her premature twin cousins, given that she is an atheist. Nevertheless, I felt that my conduct was held to account by colleagues because I was ordained. Even as I struggled with their expectations, I held myself to account far more. The contrast between being Jenny, whom they had known and worked with for a number of years, and, I think, respected as a good person to have around, and being Jenny, who is not only a Christian, but also a priest, was hard to bear at times. I knew at one level that projection would have been part of that dynamic, but it did not make it any easier to find my way through the minefields that kept opening up in front of me.

Keeping it all going

In August 2007, I started my training course, part-time, while continuing to work full-time. By early 2008, I was journaling about the difficulty in keeping everything going. Reading through the entries, the difficulties stem in part, not surprisingly, from the pressure on my time, but also from the emotional and spiritual demands I was experiencing:

> I'm becoming more and more aware that I need to be less of a "doer"—to allow myself time to reflect and grow. Yet I think a lot of this happens for me as I read and as I plan things. I'm not sure how sitting around doing nothing will improve things!

By June 2008, I was doing a church placement, and writing frequently about feeling overwhelmed, and about needing to get the work-life balance more equal. I noted that I felt greedy for opportunities, to experience as many different ways as possible in which ministry could be exercised, while at the same time wanting to continue to do my professional, secular work as well as I always had. By late August, I was well into both my church placement and my placement with a hospital chaplain, I had been to summer school, and I had delivered a daughter and car full of her belongings to Amsterdam where she was going to study for an MA. Returning to work after a period of leave to allow me to do all these things, I wrote, wryly, that one of my colleagues had asked me if I had had a good break!

In September, following a weekend away on my training course, I came home to an empty house (my husband was away), and no voice—the one thing that could prevent me from doing my job as a teacher. I took time off work, feeling guilty because I was not working from home, but was in bed. Writing that now, I wonder what was the matter with me, that I could not rest even when feeling quite unwell?!

Following my ordination as a deacon in June 2009, I was plunged back into working out how to balance ministry and work. Just over a fortnight in, my training incumbent told me on the Monday morning that I was preaching the following Sunday—but Monday was my one day, apart from Sunday, for ministry and I already had a full day planned, so when was I going to prepare a sermon? By Friday evening:

> I am at that stage where all the world seems to be against me, and I could burst into tears at the slightest provocation.
>
> I feel strongly the pull of wanting to get stuck into all this, especially when [my training incumbent] talks of ways he would like to move things forward. And yet I know I have to take time to get into the routine of it, to gain general experience. I think it's also important to work out what it means to be a deacon in the [workplace].

I realized that no one else was going to provide a structure for me, either to help with time management, or to work out what my new identity meant. I clearly felt "a bit at sea", not sure what I was supposed to be doing in the parishes, trying to work out "logistical problems . . . like arranging who to visit and where to make phone calls from", and where to spend bits of spare time—I did not live in the parishes I was placed in, and had no obvious home there. None of this was helped by the fact that I planned to be in the parishes Sundays and Mondays, because by then I worked four days a week in my secular job, Tuesday to Friday, but my training incumbent's day off was a Monday!

Looking after myself better was a frequent theme in these journal entries, as was tiredness, and worrying about too great a workload, both in my secular job and in the parish. Time management was a perennial problem at that stage for me, with the demands of my job, and the demands of being a curate. By January 2010, I was concerned that I was being expected to do more work in my secular employment than was possible in the number of hours I worked, and was in discussion with others about where I should be prioritizing my time: "At least everyone has recognized that my time can't be accounted more than 100 per cent." In addition, one of our parish ministry team had needed to take time off since Christmas Eve with a back injury, and I found myself telling my training incumbent that I simply could not continue the workload he seemed to be expecting of me, and that I felt he was doing far too much himself. I was feeling tired and frustrated with it all, and felt that I was being used rather than trained. After a visit to my sick colleague, I wrote that "on the one hand we want to be supportive, and on the other comes looking after ourselves"; I needed time with my training incumbent to address issues of time off and boundaries. Another problem was evening meetings, which tended not to end until after 9pm, and after which I would have at least twenty minutes' drive home to an empty house,[16] probably not yet having eaten, because I had gone to the meeting straight from work.

The year from summer 2011 to summer 2012 featured stress, exhaustion and shingles. I began to see all this as an indication that I was trying to do too much, and that I needed to do something about it. I eventually dropped to three days a week at my secular job, and started to plan for early retirement, which took place at Easter 2013. Even so, in November 2013 I was noting in my journal, for the *n*th time, how hard it was to restrict my parish ministry to the time allocated for it—on non-ministry days that week, I was accompanying someone to a difficult solicitor's meeting and taking a funeral—while trying to keep my freelance professional work going, and my professional doctorate: "I know I need to be more firm about boundaries if I'm to honour my commitment in these areas. Yet how can I ignore people who need what I can offer . . . ".

Subsequent entries talk about the need for an action plan to ensure that I did not lose sight of anything that I was committed to doing: Christmas was approaching, with its overload of services to prepare, plus I wanted to plan a day out with my husband, noting that if I started thinking I did not have time for it, then it was definitely "time to take a step back"! I ended up in bed for twenty-four hours, not because I was actually ill, but because I badly needed time out. My workload was compounded by family issues to do with my elderly father, who had been in hospital, and was not able to return to his own home on his own any more, and the birth of my first grandchild, which was a difficult one, necessitating a stay in hospital of about a fortnight for my daughter before and after the birth, and several days in the NICU for my grandson.

I felt that I was in a wilderness place, where I was very aware of my vulnerabilities, especially where my family was concerned. I was driving back and forth from home to visit my daughter and grandson, and my father—a round trip of over 165 miles—and was becoming increasingly exhausted. The physical toll on my energy was compounded by the emotional toll. Nevertheless, immediately after Christmas I went out to South Africa to teach again. It reaffirmed me in my identity as a teacher, and thus as a PSW, as I recognized yet again how much it was "a two-way street" between my secular work and my ministry.

Coming up to date

The story that I have told so far makes it sound as if there was a lot of struggle and not much joy in my PSW journey, which is not the case. There were many joys along the way, not least the privileges of leading worship and listening to people talk about their lives and their faith. In focusing on my struggle to recognize and grow into my own vocation as a PSW, I have tried to point the way to issues of identity and context which any theological model for the PSW must encompass.

I realize that I do not actually know when I did my last work as a maths educator. I made a decision not to return to South Africa, then prevaricated about it. In the end, I did not return after January 2015 because, for a couple of years, other things got in the way. I thought seriously about going out in January 2019, but, with the deadline for my professional doctorate looming, decided that was a bad idea. In the summer of 2019, I finally confirmed my decision to let that go when I was asked to participate in ongoing collaboration with other colleagues who had been part of that work, and declined. I have no idea now when my last workshop in the UK was! When I wrote the first draft of this chapter, I said that maths education and I had now parted company—it turns out that this is not the case, however. One of my grandsons, with his parents, is in the USA and is currently being home-schooled partly because of uncertainties about where they will settle, and partly because of the way in which the COVID-19 pandemic there has impacted schools. I am now his "maths teacher" from afar, recording videos and suggesting activities for him to do to supplement the diet of worksheets available online. I note that I am enjoying the challenge of it—I have never home-schooled a child, nor taught a five-year-old—and am excited by thinking about conceptual learning at his stage, and how to encourage and develop it!

Just as my secular work has changed considerably since 2009, when I was ordained, so too has the focus of my church-based ministry. I left my second group of parishes on Trinity Sunday 2019, and was licensed at Ely Cathedral as Minister for Social Justice (self-supporting) shortly afterwards. My ministry is now all about justice for people and for the environment, and is taking me into many places I could not have imagined back in 2009. As I wrote this, a small group of us were considering the practicalities of building up the community support group we set up at the start of the pandemic lockdown in March 2020 to become some kind of food co-operative. With other people, I am looking at how we might build awareness and support agencies trying to combat modern slavery and exploitative work in our area, and how we can implement planning for becoming carbon neutral by 2030 both at Ely Cathedral and in Ely Diocese.

—

I believe in the church and in parish ministry, but I also believe there is room for other ways to be church and to be a priest which, while rooted in the worship and work of the parish, are about being part of Christ's kingdom in the wider world. In Part 1 of this book, I set out the context for my theological model of the PSW, the research that I did, and the voices that I listened to which helped me to construct a conceptual framework for the PSW. In Part 2, I use the words of my interviewees to set out PSW narratives and to conceptualize a theological model for the PSW, the priest in secular work.

Part 1: The Context

On a course in the autumn of 2009, I took my morning coffee into a library which held a number of books about non-stipendiary ministry. Idly flicking through one or two of them, I read about men in the 1970s who were ordained to be non-stipendiary priests, who would continue to work in their secular jobs, while also contributing to parish ministry. What caught my eye was a discussion of the difficulty these men experienced in holding their secular work and their parish ministry together—in tension.

As I described in the previous chapter, I was struggling with adjusting to being a deacon while continuing my secular work. Reading Hodge's report in that library that day, I realized two things: that I needed to find ways to answer my questions about what it meant to be such a person, and that answering them might be helpful to other people in similar situations.[17] Soon after starting my research in the autumn of 2012, I revisited Hodge's report, and could not find anything that specifically mentioned holding the tension, and yet that phrase had lodged in my memory. I can only conclude this actually described my own experience, which resonated sufficiently with that of the 1970s NSMs for me to attribute it to Hodge's account.

Twenty-eight PSWs took part in my original research, and I have had informal conversations with many more since then—if you are someone I have talked to at any stage, thank you, I am very grateful to you all. The combination of parish and secular work for each PSW is unique and easily recognizable by those who know (of) them. In order to maintain the anonymity of my participants, I therefore do not give individual details.

My focus in this part of the book is on the context which is the background to the theological model of the PSW. In order to present a case for enlarging the church's understanding of the nature of this particular form of priestly ministry, in the hope that it will be recognized as the significant and unique gift that it is, the lived experience of PSWs and their self-understanding needs to be situated in its theological context. Given the lack of understanding or recognition in many parts of the institutional church, the voice of the academy is a necessary foundation for making the case for the particular vocation of the PSW. Chapter 2 therefore outlines the theological context, particularly the role of the church in the world and in this age (the *saeculum*), discussing what "sacred" and "secular" mean, and leading into the theology of the *missio Dei*. In Chapter 3, I give a brief account of how our current understanding of ordained priesthood has evolved from the late nineteenth century onwards, which acts as a basis for the discussion in Chapter 4 of models of priesthood. In Chapter 5, I consider what it means "to have a vocation". In Chapter 6, I describe the research I have carried out.

CHAPTER 2

Theological context: Between Pentecost and the Parousia

During my exploration of theological literature, and as I now reflect on why I have chosen the authors and subjects that I have, I have discovered much about myself. This has truly been a personal journey of discovery, and the choices I have made in selecting particular theologians and authors with whom to dialogue, and particular theological areas on which to focus, depend on that personal journey. Although I started my research as a way of wrestling with my own self-understanding in order to achieve some kind of coherence about who and what I think I am, over time it became clear to me that I was not alone, and that it would be helpful if I could articulate a shared self-understanding, based on multiple voices, for those of us for whom my designation of PSW is not only appropriate, but contains something important about our self-understanding. There are many theological areas which might be considered relevant. In this chapter, I focus on the period between Pentecost and the Parousia—the age, or *saeculum*, of the church—and the church's participation in the *missio Dei*.

Since Pentecost, two millennia have passed, and the world has changed. During that time, there have been periods when it would have made no sense at all to differentiate between what is labelled "sacred" and what is labelled "secular". In our own age, however, even though we might agree that everything is sacred because part of God's world, these concepts need some discussion. We pray regularly that God's kingdom will come on earth as in heaven, recognizing that the kingdom is both present and still to come, that it is eschatological and that creation is not yet fully part of Christ's kingdom. The church, Christ's body on earth in this age, is both part of the kingdom and part of what is not yet the kingdom, so both sacred and secular, as is every other aspect of life here and now.

Writing to his baby godson on the occasion of the child's baptism, Dietrich Bonhoeffer described the church as fighting "only for its self-preservation, as though that were an end in itself", making it "incapable of taking the world of reconciliation and redemption to mankind [sic] and the world". He went on to say that the church had thus lost its right to speak, and needed to find "a new language, perhaps quite non-religious, but liberating and redeeming".[18] All the participants in my research, in one way or another, talked of the need to find ways to communicate with people in their own contexts, and not simply from inside the church. Although they all challenged the use of the word "secular" as a way to describe their vocation, claiming that all life belongs to God and that their work outside the church was every bit as sacred as their work inside it, they too saw a need for a new language, a different way to connect with people, which would start from where people are located. As one participant put it, the significance of the PSW is that their ministry "is not merely non-stipendiary, it's secular". I use "secular" in PSW to qualify the work the PSW does which is outside the institutional church, but, with my participants, I make the claim that the PSW's "secular work" contributes to the *missio Dei*.

The church and the world, sacred and secular

Bonhoeffer cautioned against thinking in terms of two separate spheres, where one is "divine, supernatural and Christian" and the other is "worldly, profane, natural and un-Christian".[19] Such separation suggests that there is a reality which exists beyond God's reach, which is a "secular existence which can claim autonomy for itself and can exercise this right of autonomy in its dealings with the spiritual sphere".[20] This is contradictory to the claims of scripture, that "in him all things in heaven and on earth were created" (Colossians 1:16). As a consequence, Bonhoeffer affirmed that "there is only one sphere" in which "we stand at once in both the reality of God and the reality of the world".[21]

In the Revelation, John of Patmos described two cities, which will only be separated at the Parousia. Babylon is a symbol of idolatry, self-glorification and violence (Revelation 18), which although clearly code for Rome, is also a symbol or a parable for any city, nation or institution which is under the threat of death;[22] the new Jerusalem, on the other hand, is symbolic of the redeemed people of God (Revelation 21:1–4). Augustine used Babylon and Jerusalem as types for the two cities of *De civitate Dei*—*civitas terrena* and *civitas Dei*, the cities of earth and of God—which, as in the parable of the wheat and the weeds (Matthew 13:24–30), are inseparable until Christ returns to judge between them.

By the time of Augustine, in the fifth century CE, Christians were using the Latin *saeculum* to denote this age, the time of the church, between Pentecost and Christ's return in the Parousia. Augustine divided history (time since the Fall) into six *saecula*, or ages, corresponding to the six days of creation, but the ultimate significance of the incarnation collapses the previous five ages into one, so that there is the time of promise (before Christ), and the time of fulfilment.[23] He characterized this age as the period of both the *civitas terrena* (or Babylon) and the *civitas Dei* (or Jerusalem), with Jesus' parable of the wheat and weeds in Matthew 13:24–30 used to explain their relationship. Because they are different in nature, but inseparable during this age, both the church and the world contain both cities: the *civitas Dei* is not to be found solely in the church, nor the *civitas terrena* solely in the world outside the church.[24] This is different from apocalyptic interpretations of the church, in which it is seen as an oasis of holiness, already chosen by God, and waiting to be set free from an alien and hostile world.[25] In the *saeculum*, the *civitas terrena* and the *civitas Dei* cannot be separated, so that "secular", meaning "of this age", and "sacred" cannot be separated either.

In his collection of essays on Augustine, Rowan Williams' analysis is that Augustine was not suggesting that there are "two distinct kinds of human association, the sacred and the secular, or even the private and the public", but that his focus was "the goal of human life as such".[26] While both cities will experience the "same vicissitudes of earth life and make use of the same temporal goods",[27] they are destined for different ends. It is in the *civitas Dei* that human beings can offer themselves to God, which for Augustine is their *raison d'être*, whereas in the *civitas terrena*, human beings are subject to the coercive power of fallen people and institutions.[28]

The fundamental intertwining of the sacred and the secular is beautifully illustrated by a diary entry of Etty Hillesum, a Jew from a non-religious family in Amsterdam, who died at the age of twenty-nine in Auschwitz. She wrote about finding herself "suddenly . . . kneeling on the brown coconut matting in the bathroom, my head hidden in my dressing gown, which was slung over the broken cane chair".[29] For her, this was a source of embarrassment, "because of the critical, rational, atheistic bit that is part of me as well", and yet "every so often I have a great urge to kneel down with my face in my hands and in this way to find some peace and to listen to that hidden source within me". Sacred moments can happen in the most unlikely places, not least in places normally deemed "secular".

However, writing in the *Church Times* in 2018, Eve Poole claimed that "because God made the world, and Christ redeemed it, there can be no secularity".[30] To illustrate what she meant, she used the examples of St Paul's sermon on the Unknown God at the Areopagus (Acts 17:16–34), the "rebranding" of Eostre as Easter and "the conversion of the goddess Brigid to a saint", claiming that these exemplify "the Christian tradition of baptizing the secular to claim it for God". If something requires baptism in order to claim it for God, that suggests that rather than there being no secularity, there is a real need to explore the distinction between "sacred" and "secular" at greater depth.

If "secular" denotes the things of this age, what do we mean by "sacred"? Early in the twentieth century, the German Lutheran theologian, Rudolf Otto, coined the word "numinous" from the Latin *numen*, meaning "divine power".[31] The "numinous" cannot be strictly defined and is non-rational and non-sensory, but it can be known through experience. Otto did not restrict the numinous to Christian religious experience, but to anything perceived to be wholly other, simultaneously mysterious, terrifying and fascinating.[32] Such ideas form part of apophatic theology, a tradition which acknowledges the impossibility of saying anything accurate about God, other than what God is not.

The Romanian historian of religions, Mircea Eliade, used Otto's ideas to form his own theory, that religions are based on "hierophanies"—events or objects where something of a "wholly different order" is experienced, which form the basis of religions, and are also a means of categorizing experience as sacred or profane.[33] Profane is not quite the same as secular, of course: the origin of the word "profane" is "outside the temple", whereas, as we have seen, the origin of the word "secular" is "of this age", a period when what is sacred (so inside the temple, metaphorically at least) is inseparable from what is profane. Eliade claimed that our experience of holy ground means that space is not homogeneous, and that there is on the one hand sacred space, which is "a strong, significant space", and on the other hand, spaces which "are not sacred and so are without structure or consistency" and are "amorphous".[34] He contrasted sacred space, which provides "orientation in the chaos of homogeneity", with profane space, which is entirely relative.[35] Moses' encounter with God in the burning bush (Exodus 3:5) is an example of sacred space, in which Moses not only meets with God, but has to respond in some way. Profane space makes no such demands.

What Eliade was trying to do was to draw out commonalities in religious experience, and to show that experience of what we call the divine is independent of culture and religion. We experience the sacred, recognizing it as other, and through sacred myths we access our origins, our creation: "Everything that the gods or the ancestors did, hence everything that the myths have to tell about their creative activity, belongs to the sphere of the sacred and therefore participates in *being*."[36]

There are various ways in which we might critique Otto's and Eliade's theories. Reading Eliade, I find my head spinning with esoteric words and ideas which seem suggestive, but which I cannot actually make sense of, when I try to pin down what he is saying! Although we may recognize the concept and the existence of the numinous, it is hard to see how a physical object or an event in real time can be "wholly other". The account of Moses' encounter with God in the burning bush in Exodus 3 is certainly a hierophany, more specifically a theophany—a manifestation of the sacred, of God—but the bush remained a bush, and is therefore not "wholly other". Indeed, its very ordinariness and earthiness symbolize God's participation in the call to Moses in the real physical world, and all that followed from it.

Another critique of theories such as Eliade's is that they tend to result in reductive explanations of phenomena, often not distinguishing adequately between sacred and religious, and consequently do not provide for the many forms which the sacred can take in human experience.[37] In recognizing as sacred what someone, in a particular place at a particular time, deems sacred, Lynch, for example, replaced *a priori* conceptualizations of the sacred with a contextual approach. This need not be purely individual: Lynch described what he called a "cultural approach" as a means of communicating human experience of the transcendent through symbols which gain potency through use in collective rituals involving words, actions and emotions (so, for instance, laying poppy wreaths at Remembrance services).[38]

By the end of the twentieth century, it was common, in the secular west at least, to assert that an object or place is not sacred in and of itself, as Eliade had claimed, but is sacred only if someone claims that for it.[39] This is indicative of a post-modern tendency to minimize, ignore or refute any claims for absolutes, which, for the American scholar of religions, Robert Orsi, results in a "deep antipathy between modern cultures all over the world and the practice and experience of sacred presence".[40] Such antipathy allows what is sacred in people's lives to be deliberately ignored, so that sacred stories are rejected as a framework through which people can tell their own stories.[41] Orsi illustrated this with an account of going into an Italian Catholic community in the USA, similar to that in which he had been brought up, to study the phenomenon of prayer to St Jude. Initially, he congratulated himself on being there to listen to people's stories, but soon found himself wondering how much "these people" actually cared what he thought of their stories or their spirituality.[42] Eventually he was challenged by a worshipper: "Have *you* even prayed to Saint Jude?", because if not, how could he understand?

There is a danger that academic study of what is deemed sacred misses the point. Orsi found himself caught between a world which he thought he understood, but of which he was no longer a part, and the academic world which wanted to liberate people from regressive, dependent views. He argued that such notions of liberation misunderstand the nature of religion, which is not about finding meaning, but about the relationship between heaven and earth, expressed through practices like that of praying to St Jude. When I read the story of Moses at the burning bush, I intuitively understand what sacred means, so I do not need to subject the story to the kind of analysis which does not accept such understanding. Similarly praying to St Jude made perfect sense to the people Orsi described, but situating himself as an analytical observer, he found himself challenged not simply by one of "these people", but by his own early experiences. It feels a bit like catching butterflies to pin them down—their essence is lost.

In contemporary usage, the idea of "sacred" is perhaps best illustrated by the roadside bunches of flowers and other objects, left as a memorial to a loss of life—places where something profound has happened, which needs to be marked in a symbolic way. Such memorials are not to be treated as roadside rubbish, to be removed and summarily disposed of, but are left to the elements. The word "secular" now means anything which is not religious, while "profane" can be used as a synonym for "secular", but also may carry nuances of irreverence, even cursing. The loss of a religious register has taken away much of the earlier meanings of these words.

Christians living in this age before the full restoration of God's kingdom might well ask with the psalmist, therefore: "How could we sing the Lord's song in a foreign land?" (Psalm 137:4). One answer is that of Revelation 21:3-4:[43]

> See, the home of God is among mortals. He will dwell with them; they will be his peoples, and God himself will be with them; he will wipe every tear from their eyes. Death will be no more; mourning and crying and pain will be no more, for the first things have passed away.

This is not purely future: the hope expressed in the New Testament is that this is already happening, that although we have no choice but to be part of the *civitas terrena*, we are also part of the *civitas Dei*. In Jeremiah 29:4-9, the prophet told the Babylonian exiles that they should make lives for themselves in Babylon, and "seek the welfare of the city where I have sent you into exile, and pray to the Lord on its behalf, for in its welfare you will find your welfare". As citizens of the *civitas Dei*, we are commanded to pray for the *civitas terrena*, and in seeking its welfare to find our own.

The church in the saeculum

The church is both part of Christ's reign and part of fallen creation, and so it is important to avoid the "lazy" ecclesiology which fails to acknowledge the reality of actual churches, as compared to theological and doctrinal statements about *the* church.[44] Stringfellow, a twentieth-century American lay theologian, lawyer and social activist, described the Fall as "*the alienation of the whole of Creation from God*, and, thus, the rupture and profound disorientation of all relationships within the whole of Creation".[45] The situation of the church in the *saeculum* is that it is subject to disorientation and death because of the Fall, but also subject to grace, because God is not absent from God's world, and in Jesus has made good that rupture and disorientation. God's kingdom is present in churches, but also in nations and institutions, through the work of the Holy Spirit; the body of Christ, which shares in the life of the new creation, is not to be equated with ecclesiastical structures now or at any other time.

Bonhoeffer acknowledged that there are valid questions to be asked about the status of the visible church and the reality of evil.[46] He answered such questions by arguing that the church is "the place where testimony and serious thought are given to God's reconciliation of the world with Himself in Christ", and that its vocation is to show the world that it (the world) has been redeemed in Christ. When it fails to live up to this vocation, it becomes "a religious society which fights in its own interest and thereby ceases at once to be the Church of God and of the world". In the *saeculum*, we have no choice but to accept that the church, like everything else, is both provisional and ambiguous, secular (of this age) as well as sacred (part of God's provision), and that the secular and sacred are inextricably intertwined. Because the kingdom exists both within and without the church, God's work in the world is only partly carried out in the church, so while the church proclaims God's kingdom, it is not that kingdom, and cannot grow into that kingdom of itself.

For Rowan Williams, living a religious life is not about being spiritual, but about living a life in which God is acknowledged, and in which a narrative which admits God's presence is an acceptable one.[47] The church is that body of people who celebrate the God who has revealed Godself to them in the person of Jesus Christ, and who—with, in and through Christ—make possible a space called the kingdom of God, anticipating its full establishment here on earth. A secular space is then one in which narratives which include God are deemed inadmissible, because they are not immediately accessible to reason and evidence.[48] The difference between understanding something as sacred or secular then depends on whether it is interpreted functionally—what you see is what you get—or whether we are prepared to allow that there may be more to it than what we currently perceive or understand (so art, for instance, is not secular because it is always more than its creator intended).

In a functionalist worldview, with its lack of any transcendent register, there is a clear danger of losing sight of the fact that people and things exist for what they are in themselves, and are more than the means to an end. For Eliade, the church is the threshold between this age and the next, the gatekeeper in effect, and is a sacred space open to heaven, symbolized by Jacob's ladder (Genesis 28:12–19).[49] For Williams, it "is . . . the trustee of a vision" even though it so often fails to live up to that vision.[50] It matters, however, that, living up to it or not, the church enshrines the vocation to notice and proclaim God's presence in the here and now.

The *missio Dei*

In the *Introduction* to his seminal work on mission, David Bosch made the assertion that mission "refers primarily to the *missio Dei* (God's mission), that is, God's self-revelation" through God's love of and involvement in the world, "in which the church is privileged to participate".[51] This is the understanding of *missio Dei* assumed here.

The language of "sending", corresponding to the Latin *mittere*, in connection with Jesus is of course scriptural (e.g. John 20:21), and although it has become associated with ecclesiology and theology of mission in past decades, the term *missio Dei* can be found as early as

Augustine's writings, with his discussion of the sending of the Son and the Holy Spirit by the Father in *De Trinitate*.[52] Recent interpretation of the *missio Dei* was first articulated by Karl Barth at the Brandenburg Mission Conference of 1932,[53] where Barth argued that because God is originally and eternally in fellowship in Godself, God could cause there to be a covenant with human beings, so that in history human beings could participate in God's triune life.[54] It is an essential property of God to be missionary, because "God in and for himself *[sic]* for and to all eternity transitions the gap between the above and the below." The Son is sent by the Father, and the Holy Spirit "transitions the partnership of the Father and the Son" and "creates a [human] community in correspondence to the God who lives his own proper life in coming to us".[55] The effect of God acting in this community is to make it into a witness to the acts of God, and so mission is part of the doctrine of the Trinity, rather than an aspect of ecclesiology or soteriology.[56]

It was the Conference on World Mission and Evangelism in Tambaram in 1938[57] which Bosch pinpointed as the critical point at which the relationship between church and mission changed, through its recognition that there was a fault line through the church, not simply between the church and the world or Christianity and paganism.[58] Between Tambaram in 1938 and the next but one meeting in Willingen in 1952,[59] there was a shift in focus from church-centred mission to a mission-centred church:

> It was recognized that the church could be neither the starting point nor the goal of mission. God's salvific work precedes both church and mission. We should not subordinate mission to the church nor the church to mission; both should, rather be taken up into the *missio Dei*, which now became the overarching concept. The *missio Dei* institutes the *missiones ecclesiae*. The church changes from being the sender to being the one sent.[60]

On the Conference on World Mission and Evangelism website, it is claimed that "Willingen is rightly considered to have had the most lasting influence on ecumenical mission theology" and that "the idea of *missio Dei*, that was taken up in the follow-up to Willingen, proved to be most creative".[61] Part of the background to the new thinking of Willingen came from Bonhoeffer's metaphor for the church as a pilgrim people, based on the image of Israel in the wilderness and prominent in 1 Peter (e.g. 2:11) and Hebrews (e.g. 11:13).[62] The church has no permanent place in which to abide in the world, but is always *en route* to the kingdom of God, and so the "church is the church only when it exists for others . . . The church must share in the secular problems of ordinary human life".[63]

The emphasis on "a missionary ecclesiology of the local church" was confirmed during the work of Vatican II with the publication of *Lumen gentium* in 1964.[64] In *Lumen gentium*, the church is seen as receiving "the mission to proclaim and to spread among all peoples the Kingdom of Christ and of God".[65] By 1965, *Ad gentes*, another document emerging from Vatican II, was an attempt "to sketch the principles of missionary activity and to rally the forces of the faithful", given "the present state of affairs, out of which there is arising a new situation for mankind *[sic]*".[66]

In *Ad gentes*, the *missio Dei* is defined as the self-expression of God the Trinity, flowing out in love to all people, with the church and the church's mission deriving from that.[67] As a consequence, it is serving God through serving God's world and pointing to God's activity in that world which is primary, with planting churches and saving souls following from that.[68] The lesson we should learn from the Acts of the Apostles is that the church needs to respond to local contexts, and so it will continually be reinventing itself as it crosses new boundaries.[69]

Early in the twenty-first century, echoing Augustine's view that the church is not coterminous with the kingdom, Moltmann claimed that the responsibility for mission does not rest simply on church leadership, or those with a designation of missionary or pioneer. Moltmann's argument was that the world's salvation does not lie specifically within the church, so "churchifying" the world is not the answer. Rather it is for the church to serve and help to bring about the coming salvation of the world.[70] Because this responsibility lies with the whole body of Christ, the corollary of the church's *raison d'être* being mission is that there is need of a sound theology of the laity.[71]

In 1982, *Baptism, Eucharist and Ministry*,[72] the Lima text of the World Council of Churches, had emphasized that the gifts of the Spirit are given for the whole church, to enable it to participate in the *missio*

Dei. Christians become part of the *missio Dei* through their baptism, in which they are made part of the eschatological community which is working with the Holy Spirit to redeem creation.[73] Because the entire church represents Christ, the role of the priest is therefore not to work on behalf of the church, but rather to work alongside everyone in the church in and with the community. Lay people need not be trained as "mini-pastors",[74] but rather the ministry they have in their communities and places of work should be taken seriously. In 2007, in *Mission and Ministry*, the Faith and Order Advisory Group of the Church of England agreed that "the mission of the Son and the Spirit creates the Church and the Church only exists in relation to the *missio Dei*",[75] echoing the earlier work of the Conference of World Mission and Evangelism at Willingen.

None of this was new, as can be seen from the 1549 Second Collect for Good Friday, but was in need of renewed recognition.

> Almighty and everlasting God, by whose Spirit the whole body of the Church is governed and sanctified; Receive our supplications and prayers which we offer before thee for all estates of men [sic] in thy holy Church, that every member of the same, in his vocation and ministry, may truly serve thee; through our Lord . . .[76]

Given the developments in biblical studies and ecumenical engagement, together with significant changes in British society in the second half of the twentieth century, *Mission and Ministry* asked what kind of ministry would be required for the missionary task before the church in the early twenty-first century, recognizing that we cannot simply transfer practice in the New Testament to today's Britain. While acknowledging the need for contextual interpretation of scripture, the analysis that followed was based on the threefold order of bishops, priests and deacons, with a separate laity, however. The implication is that although the church should take account of how life in Britain in general is changing, the basic structure and orders of the church can still be taken as given.

In an important study on collaborative ministry, Stephen Pickard, an Australian theologian and bishop, suggested that a "relational approach to ministry" should be grounded in what we know of God, so that we base our ecclesiology on the Trinity, and only then think about what that implies for the church's ministry.[77] He claimed that despite much being written and said, "the work of transposition and interweaving of Trinitarian and relational categories into an ecclesiology of ministry remains significantly underdeveloped".[78] Apostolic succession proceeding from Christ to his apostles and hence to today's bishops need not be axiomatic, but should be seen as passing to the body of Christ, the whole church.

There is a tension between the church seen as "the sole bearer of a message of salvation" and the church as "an illustration—in word and deed—of God's involvement with the world".[79] These extremes are not mutually exclusive however, and need to be held together in balance. One way of describing such a balance is to see the church as "an ellipse with two foci": one focus is its prayer and worship, the other is its engagement with, and challenge of, the world. It is only possible for the church to engage in mission if it is different from the world, yet also in the world; the church is simultaneously both part of the *missio Dei* and also in need of setting its own house in order, and so an object of the *missio Dei*.[80]

The purpose of the church is, like that of John the Baptist, to point beyond itself to God. It is not therefore irrelevant or redundant, far from it. God is the primary agent, but the church is God's chosen partner, instituted by Christ and, insofar as its life is breathed through by the Holy Spirit, an instrument of the *missio Dei*.

CHAPTER 3

How did we get here? A brief history

> The official preservation of the Christian faith and the formal continuity of the church have always been in danger of becoming the ultimate concern in the church at the expense of the continuing experience of this faith in different times and cultural circumstances.[81]

This quotation forms a useful backdrop to an account of how we arrived at the current position. In 1983, Hodge's report on non-stipendiary ministry in the 1970s claimed that "the reluctance to encourage variation from the parochial model of ministry is a recurring feature in [the] history" of non-stipendiary ministry.[82] The fact that I have felt the need to write this book is an indication of the lack of attention paid to models of ministry other than the parochial model in the decades that followed.

According to the New Testament, St Paul was at least partly a self-supporting apostle, generally described as a tentmaker (Acts 18:3). However, by the time that the Church of England came into being in the sixteenth century, a person in holy orders was only permitted:

> ... to be gainfully employed in a school, as a publisher, as a manager of a life assurance society, or in farming up to 80 acres, [and was] specifically prohibited ... from engaging in any trade or dealing for gain in any goods, wares or merchandize.[83]

Bishops were instructed not to allow their clergy to engage in any other kind of work, with the effect that the only realistic options for the vast majority of ordained men[84] were to be a farmer, schoolmaster or university don.

In his report, Hodge listed a number of key events which brought about change during the period between the First World War and the 1970s. The first was the war itself, which resulted not only in a lack of men able to offer themselves for ordination, but also in an overall feeling of being in a new and unknown situation. In 1912, Roland Allen, a missionary in North China, had advocated the case for "tentmaker" ministry like that of the apostle Paul. Back in Britain, responding to the post-war sense of crisis, Allen continued to press the case for what he called "voluntary ministry".[85] By the early 1930s, permission was given for bishops to ordain so-called volunteer priests, but in such a way that they were discouraged from actually doing so.[86]

Times were changing, however. The Lambeth Conference of 1930, although it did not materially advance the cause of voluntary priesthood, did at least put it on the agenda, and gradually more prophetic voices echoed Allen's lead. Among them were three bishops who were significant in changing the mindset of the church: Russell Barry (Southwell, 1941–63), Michael Ramsey (Durham, and then successively Archbishop of York and of Canterbury, 1961–74) and Mervyn Stockwood (Southwark, 1959–80). Hodge also pointed to what he described as "the role of pilot projects", referring to the examples set by other Anglican provinces, notably Hong Kong.[87]

The situation following the Second World War was similar to that after the First in that there was again a sense of needing new ways forward, combined with a shortage of candidates for ordination. Although the 1932 Convocation of Canterbury had concluded that "We are unable to recommend, in normal cases, the ordination of men [sic] to the priesthood unless they can give their whole time to ministerial work",[88] by 1955 a Convocation of Canterbury report claimed that "some clergy were currently engaged in [secular] occupations to augment inadequate incomes", and that a more flexible approach would supplement parochial ministry, bridge the gap between industry and the church, and enable pastoral care in the secular world to be more effective.[89] Nevertheless, throughout the 1950s, despite concerns about the effectiveness of ministry in the secular world, and the financial situation of the clergy, the emphasis was still very much on parochial ministry, with the Report[90] observing that the "tradition of a *parochial* ministry . . . is so ingrained in our history and our thinking that we find it hard to consider alternative possibilities *de novo*". The Report was prepared to consider such possibilities, however, continuing that it was "essential that the character and function of these alternative ministries should be thought out, at the outset, without continual reference to the extent to which they can supplement the work of the parish priest", and recommending that anyone ordained to this ministry "should not be regarded as an unpaid curate", but that "he *[sic]* should be left free to deal pastorally with the people who are already known to him in the course of his secular work".

It is evident that things were changing, and, in 1959, Canon C28 was revised to allow clergy to engage in secular work under the authority and licence of their diocesan bishop.[91] Canon C28 is still in force today in the same form as in 1959:

> C 28 Of the occupations of ministers
> 1. No minister holding ecclesiastical office shall engage in trade or any other occupation in such manner as to affect the performance of the duties of his *[sic]* office, except so far as he be authorized so to do under the statutory provisions in this behalf for the time being in force or he have a licence so to do granted by the bishop of the diocese.[92]

In 1960, Allen's 1930 book on voluntary ministry was reprinted—its time was coming. Seeing this as a happy ending to the story would be premature however. It would be easy to gain the impression from Hodge, reporting in 1983, that NSM, and in particular the ministry of those also employed in secular work, was doomed to failure. One reported reason was the perception that an ordained person in the workplace is no different from any other Christian in that context, so there was no need to ordain people if they were not going into full-time parish ministry; another was the difficulty for both lay and ordained in exercising any kind of ministry in the workplace beyond that of pastoral care.[93] Some of Hodge's respondents found that they became less interested in their secular jobs, while others were very concerned about the appropriate use of time, insisting that their parish ministry should not get in the way of doing their secular jobs properly. Some respondents reported reluctance on the part of their incumbents to involve them fully in parish life, including Sunday worship. More positively, Hodge recorded some respondents valuing the extended contact with non-churchgoers and non-Christians, causing them to work through hard questions deriving from hard circumstances, and, in so doing, enriching their parish ministry.

Nothing much had changed when, in 1990, Hacking, then a Church of England priest, wrote *A Vision for Non-Stipendiary Ministry*. In his Foreword, George Carey admitted that while he did not "need convincing of the value of the non-stipendiary minister", he was "very concerned that over the last ten years or so it seems we have lost our way".[94] In a prescient paragraph, Hacking observed that what was more worrying was "the capacity to force what may well indeed be a genuine new development into an existing mould", commenting that "there is . . . considerable resistance to this being anything other than some kind of 'back-up' to the existing form and shape of the Church, in which NSMs can be seen as the answer to the problem of shortage of clergy and money."[95]

Following a survey of self-supporting ministers (SSMs) conducted in 2010, Teresa Morgan highlighted many of the issues reported by Hodge. Although she noted considerable progress on issues to do with initial training and training during curacy, the "disempowerment and marginalization of NSMs in their own parishes"[96] shows little change from Hodge's observations. In 1983, Hodge had recorded that:

> Non-stipendiary ministry's potential mission to society has no doubt been inhibited by the traditional understanding of priestly ministry which is part of our cultural heritage. It is the parochial model which remains dominant in the minds of us all—non-stipendiary and stipendiary clergy, lay Church members, and in society at large.[97]

In 2010, Morgan wrote that:

> The lack of any policy, and the often-repeated comment by respondents that they feel ignored, overlooked or under-used, suggest strongly that the current picture is not one of stability but of stagnation. Far too often, it seems, dioceses train ordinands—at

considerable expense—ordain them and place them in a parish or chaplaincy, and then simply forget about them.[98]

During the 1980s, the proportion of ministers in the Church of England in some form of SSM varied between 20 per cent and 30 per cent, and that remains the case still.[99] This means that throughout the past thirty years or so, on average roughly one in four ordained ministers in the Church of England has been SSM, many of them also in some kind of secular work—the Church has yet to move beyond treating them as stop-gaps to prop up parish ministry, and has yet to recognize adequately their distinctive contribution. This is not simply about personnel management or resourcing the Church; as Hacking pointed out, it goes right to the heart of what the Church believes about itself and its ministry. Hacking claimed that the Church's failure to think through such issues derived from a lack of thought "about how the Church understands the relationship of God and the creation", asking: "Just what sort of God do we believe in? What is God's will for a world such as ours at this time? And what sort of ministry is appropriate to communicate, proclaim and incarnate these beliefs?"[100]

In May 2013, a celebration of, and consultation on, SSM was held in Southwark Cathedral to mark the fiftieth anniversary of the first ordinations of NSMs from the Southwark Ordination Course. Among the blessings noted were "richness of experience that comes from diverse backgrounds", "engaging with the real world and the opportunities that brings", "being a bridge between church and world", "freedom from needs of the institution", "we can walk alongside people", and "freedom . . . to be on the fringe". Among the problems noted were "limited use of SSM gifts", "definition of role—try to be squeezed into a parochial traditional pattern", and the need for "remodelling the church to embrace the different models/experiences of ministry". The report further highlighted "being liminal and therefore connected", "freedom to be a different kind of priest", and "allowed to be ourselves, including among work colleagues". These quotations were taken from a report issued by Ministry Division at the time; it is, however, no longer available on the Church of England website.[101]

This may now (September 2020) be changing. A number of recent developments are described in the Postscript, with a comment that we may just possibly be at a *kairos* moment.

CHAPTER 4

Models of priesthood

Dominant theology of priesthood in the Church of England

There is no single theology of priesthood in the Church of England. We can, however, distinguish two significant strands. In one, it is the identity of the priest which is emphasized; in the other, the focus is on the priesthood of the church or of all believers.

In his seminal work put together from his charges to ordinands, Ramsey asked the question: "why the priest?"[102] Unsurprisingly, given the context, Ramsey focused on the individual priest, who, he argued, needed to be a theologian, a minister of reconciliation, a man [sic] of prayer, and a man of the Eucharist. The priest is not simply a (or even the) means by which the ministry of Christ is made apparent in the here and now, but, like the church, is Christ's gift to the world. At ordination, the bishop ordains priests into the Church of God, to share in the ministry of the gospel of Christ. They are given authority to bless and absolve in Christ's name. The priest displays, enables and contributes to the church's character and mission.

Ramsey was following a tradition set by Bishop Moberly in 1897 with the publication of *Ministerial Priesthood*,[103] and reinforced by its reissue in 1969. In the *Introduction* to the reissue, the key question for Moberly is identified as: "How is the church's ministry authorized?"[104] The immediate context of Moberly's apologia was threefold: the "Erastianism whereby the Church was regarded as a department of State in a confidently Christian society";[105] the rejection of Anglican orders in 1896 by Pope Leo XIII in *Apostolicae curae*; and more functionalist understandings of priestly ministry from some parts of the Church of England.[106] Moberly's answer to the question was that the church's ministry did not rest upon the authority of either the state or Rome, but on Christ through the mechanism of apostolic succession.

Although Moberly did not understand the priest as Christ's direct substitute, neither did he see ordination as purely functional, but regarded ordination as a setting apart of men *[sic]* in which an indelible character was conferred. He asserted that the church's priesthood is primary, because the church is the body of Christ, and so baptism is the sacrament which admits a person to divine citizenship. The priest is then an organ of the body through which the body performs certain functions, not someone who stands between Christ and his body. The office of the priest is thus representative rather than vicarious (meaning a substitute). With its republication in 1969, *Ministerial Priesthood* continued to be influential, arguably forming the basis for the Church of England's understanding of the priestly office through much of the twentieth century.[107]

Moberly's focus on Christ, the founder of the church and whose representative the priest is, is a Christological interpretation of what it means to be a priest, which underlies theologies of priesthood which emphasize the role of the priest at the expense of that of the laity, losing any sense that the priest is also one of the *laos*.[108] This led Greenwood in 1994 to claim that the Church of England had fallen under the sway of a "foundational myth", in which the church is seen as "divinely-established . . . founded in prescriptive detail by Christ", with the commission to the twelve named apostles handed down to their successors, and then through apostolic succession to current day bishops and the clergy whom they ordain.[109] He argued that the consequence of this was to entrench clerical control, effectively disabling attempts by the laity to find a real voice, and so contributing to the overall lack of influence of the church outside its own structures, despite challenges to clerical control, not least through the emergence of charismatic forms of worship from the 1960s onwards.

The identification of the priest with Christ is at the root of some opposition to the priestly ministry of women. The title of a collection of essays, *Presiding Like a Woman*, challenges such identification.[110] In the *Introduction*, the editors, Slee and Burns, suggest that this asks questions about the nature of the ecclesial community, and, further, about what we mean when we designate something "holy" or "sacred". This was something I also discovered: when I started my research, I thought I was going to research the nature of a particular model of priestly ministry, but I soon realized that this would necessitate thinking about the nature of church, and so about Christ's institution of the church, and beyond that, the nature of God. As I reflect on their title now, I wonder what it means to preside like a secular worker. The identity of the priest should not matter, surely, any more than their gender should, and yet there is something about offering the people's work at the altar which is not often recognized, a point to which I return in Part 2 of this book.

A Christological starting point, if it implies that the priest is standing in for Christ, separates priest and lay, and by extension, church and world, setting up a binary opposition. It emphasizes that the church is defined through its ordained ministry, with ordained and lay qualitatively different in some way. However, if instead we start from a pneumatological stance, in which the gifting of all Christians by the Holy Spirit suggests that ministry need no longer be restricted, but could be an opportunity for all, lay as well as ordained, to exercise their gifts, that is not problem-free either.[111] If ministry arises through the gifts of all, lay and ordained, then it may be that ordination loses its point. How we understand the relationship between ordained and lay ministry is an important aspect of how the church perceives itself, and how it is perceived from outside. Where difference is emphasized, boundaries are strengthened, resulting in differentiated ministries, and a clear sense of how different orders relate to each other—but with a strong tendency to see lay ministry as subservient to ordained. Where the emphasis is on equality, boundaries are weakened, ministries and roles become more flexible. More collaborative forms of ministry are then possible, in which no one role is necessarily subservient—but as many have discovered, collaborative ministry is easier in theory than in practice!

Other twentieth-century models of priesthood

Between 1943 and 1954, some French priests left parish ministry to work in low-paid manual jobs.[112] This originated when, in 1942/3, French workers were conscripted by the German occupiers, because priests were not allowed to accompany workers into the slave camps unless they also were workers.[113] This experience provided the worker priests with a better understanding of the working class and its alienation from the church, with the result that, after the war, some chose to exercise a ministry of presence and identification by engaging in full-time manual work. Their higher level of education led many to active roles in trades unions, resulting in conflict with the church hierarchy however.[114] A lack of bridge-building with the established church meant they had no support when in 1953/4, they were suppressed by Rome, accused of being communists, and told that they could not be both workers and priests.[115]

In England at this time, similar concerns about the church's engagement with the working class resulted in the establishment of workplace chaplaincies, of which the two most significant were the South London Industrial Mission and the Sheffield Industrial Mission.[116] The underlying theology of these missions was that of "getting alongside" in a similar way to the French worker priests.[117] In Sheffield, the Director, Ted Wickham, had worked in industry prior to ordination. In 1941, he became a chaplain at a factory making bombs and shells, in the process becoming one of the Church of England clergy best "fitted to a pioneer ministry in industry".[118] His priority was forming relationships with as many different people as possible, all the while discussing "relevant Christian insights".[119] Rather than taking people out of the world into the church, he wanted them to stay put, to help in the task of changing the workplace for the better. Recognizing that a chaplain was not actually in the position of a worker, he insisted that "the creation of an informed and active laity was a priority".[120] Wickham, however, was dismissive of the parish system, and "never tried to build a bridge between industry and the Church",[121] so this initiative did not have lasting impact on the wider church. In South London, on the other hand, it was seen as desirable for worker priests to remain "parochial clergy, firmly related to the Church as it was"[122], so that they remained connected. This led to the establishment in 1963 of the Southwark Ordination Course by Bishop Mervyn Stockwood, with its aim of ordaining working men [sic] as NSMs.

The problem both for the industrial missions and for the NSMs was that congregations wanted traditional priests, who would focus full-time on the parish.¹²³ One worker priest, Jack Strong, who worked as a miner in Kent while also being vicar of a parish, found that "Conservative attitudes among a middle class contingent in the village ensured the end of the experiment."¹²⁴ The Parochial Church Council (PCC) of Strong's church complained to the bishop, essentially because of "a conflict of interests where . . . the realities of mission and ministry were bound up with a gospel and a priesthood that had to take incarnational risks in theory and practice", while "the bishop, for the sake of the survival of the institutional church and the territorial parish" saw it as more important to avoid such risks.¹²⁵ The result was that Strong was removed.

As has already been mentioned, during the 1970s, a number of men were ordained as NSMs. These were people who were already working, mainly in middle class professional jobs, which they continued post-ordination. The main impetus for this appears to have been filling gaps in the church, while recognizing that NSMs in secular employment might have a distinctive ministry in the workplace.¹²⁶ Even those NSMs who did feel that they had a specific ministry in their workplaces found it difficult to sustain, however, given the pressure they were under, with many choosing to take "early retirement or transfer to stipendiary ministry".¹²⁷

It was not only in England and France that experiments with NSMs engaged in secular work were tried; indeed, in much of the developing world there was a much greater expectation that clergy would support themselves, as local churches were in no position to do so. However, in Anglican churches the influence of British missionaries remained strong at least through the first half of the twentieth century, and the model they generally supported was that of an educated, paid clergy, despite the best efforts of missionaries like Roland Allen to encourage indigenous ministry.¹²⁸ In the Church of South India, for example, Newbigin's¹²⁹ vision for local indigenous leadership did not really embed itself, failing after his departure. Keeping secular work going while serving in the church was a problem for some, while others found that pastorate committees were not supportive of those they deemed inadequately educated, and whose social class and lifestyle were not what they expected of their clergy.¹³⁰ When the New Zealand Anglican Church tried to introduce community priests, mainly of Maori ethnicity, they found that although "cooperative ministry, natural human communities, and ministry diversity, all illustrate ways in which community priests can indeed be 'of the people'" that the structures and understanding of ministry, inherited primarily from England, tended "to mould rather relentlessly, in other directions".[131]

The issues faced by the post-war generation of worker priests and industrial missions, the NSMs of the 1970s in England, and the experience of similar experiments in ministry in other countries, demonstrate that ambiguity about the PSW vocation is not new: was it about engaging with people in the workplace, and if so, how? Or was it actually about dealing with shortages in parish ministry? In his survey of worker priests post-war, Mantle concluded that "the institutional church spoke relentlessly about mission in an industrial society, and then assessed effort and measured success by filled pews and growing territorial parishes there for everyone—if only they would come in."[132] He assessed the Church of England's ecclesiology as disabling, preventing "it from engaging with a post-Christian culture", and that "the story of Britain's first worker-priests, and those who supported them in and outside the parishes, was, and remains a judgment [sic] and challenge."[133]

Neither the worker priest nor the NSM in secular employment were able to embed their form of priestly ministry in the institutional church. The worker priests conceptualized their ministry as one of presence, walking alongside ordinary working men and, in some cases, women, but failed to take the institutional church with them; the NSMs struggled with working out what their priestly identity meant in their workplaces, other than through pastoral care or leading Bible studies or prayer groups, with the result that many transferred into full-time ministry, often taking early retirement from their secular work in order to prioritize their parish ministry.[134]

A Trinitarian approach

So far, so not good: new thinking was needed, and, perhaps surprisingly, it came from new ways of understanding God as Trinity. Rather than seeing the Trinity as some kind of union of potentially hierarchical static persons, Paul Fiddes, a Baptist theologian, focused on the mutual fellowship between Father, Son and Holy Spirit, which is symmetrical with reciprocal relationships between them.[135] He visualized this as a circle dance in which there is pattern and harmony and order: the dancers do not all do exactly the same thing at the same time, but all work together, moving into a space and then vacating it to allow another dancer into it, as they follow the rhythm of the dance. This image is dynamic, not static, providing for difference, while avoiding any suggestion that difference is permanent, or that any one participant is more important or less necessary than any other.

For Fiddes, the attraction of the dance analogy is that it keeps alive "a challenge to the image of a dominating God whose power lies in immobility and in being secure from being affected by the changing world".[136] It is not a closed dance, since we are invited to participate in the dance through "an interweaving of relational movements and actions in which we can become involved".[137] Our participation in God is eschatological, however, in that we will not know it in all fullness in this age. While we wait for the age to come, God has provided the sacraments, "pieces of earthly stuff that are meeting places with . . . God".[138] For Fiddes, one of these meeting places is the pastor, by which he means anyone who has care of others, and who points beyond themselves to God.[139]

Although Fiddes is a Baptist theologian, there are voices in the Church of England saying similar things about the Trinity and its implications for understanding priesthood. In 2014, I attended a seminar, led by a former Bishop of Grimsby, David Rossdale, in which he argued that the Christological interpretation of priesthood has had the effect of disabling the laity by allowing clericalism to flourish, and that the only way forward for the Church of England is to base its theology of priesthood on the dynamic, perichoretic Trinity.[140] A Trinitarian starting point allows us to see lay and ordained, worker priest, NSM, PSW and full-time stipendiary priest (FTS), as pastors in Fiddes' sense, who, by "daring to act for God" in their various ways, help to incarnate God in the world.[141]

CHAPTER 5

What do we mean when we talk about "having a vocation"?

When I started writing this book, I realized that it would be useful to find out more about how the process of discerning a vocation to be a PSW currently works in the Church of England. Through CHRISM[142] and through a letter which appeared in the *Church Times*,[143] I made contact with many more people, some going through the discernment process, some of them having recently passed through it, and some ordinands. The coronavirus crisis cut short my planned face-to-face interviews, so a number were facilitated by Zoom and Skype. These platforms also enabled me to go back to some people I had met with earlier on, to find out how the lockdown was affecting their work and ministry. This further research has added more detail to the picture I have constructed of the priest in secular work.

"Having a vocation" has become synonymous with feeling a sense of call to a profession such as medicine or teaching, or to some kind of ministry in the church. For the Christian, however, the primary vocation is to follow Christ, that is, to commit to being a disciple of Christ.

Here are two ways of picturing that:

In front of you is a dark forest, which you have to go through to get to where you're meant to be. You can see that there are several paths you might follow, but you can't see far enough along each one to have any idea what might lie around the next corner, never mind further in the distance. You know that you're supposed to find the right one, but how are you supposed to know? If you follow the wrong one, you won't end up where you're supposed to be, and indeed, you might find yourself somewhere you decidedly don't want to be.	In front of you are the foothills of the mountain you want to climb. You can see the top; you can also see that there are many different ways you might get there. Some look easier, at least as far as you can see, while others look harder. There's also the option of simply walking straight ahead, as far as possible, regardless of the state of the terrain underfoot. You know that if you keep following one of the paths, or keep heading towards the summit, you will eventually get there, but you don't know which would be best. You therefore set off on the route that looks most straightforward at this stage, but prepared to divert as necessary.

In the first picture, the path is already laid out, and the task of the disciple is to find it, and then follow it, avoiding wrong turnings which will lead away from the desired destination. This suggests that there is only one right way for a particular person to be a disciple, and they have to determine what that is through their interaction with God in prayer and scripture. God's promise is to guide and lead them in the way. The second picture suggests that there is a destination, but many different ways to reach that destination, some perhaps easier, some more difficult. In this scenario, the disciple does the best they can in the light of their interaction with God, recognizing that God honours the decisions they make. God's promise is to be with them in whatever comes their way.

Both are caricatures of what we mean by "vocation" of course, and it is unlikely that anyone will follow one to the exclusion of the other. Nevertheless, they do illustrate two different ways of thinking about it. For some people, it will make sense to think that God has a specific role he wants them to play in life; the task of discipleship is then to discern what it is, and get on with it. For others, it will make more sense that there is indeed a destination to be reached, but that there is more than one way to get there. God will honour the choices made, and work in and through them, even if there were better choices that might have been made, or if a choice needs to be reconsidered at any point.

The journey/path metaphor is not the only way to conceptualize vocation, however. Perhaps what we call vocation is a recognition of how we can grow more deeply into the person God created each of us to be, so coming closer to God through becoming more deeply ourselves. Our discipleship is life-long, but throughout life there are points when we realize we are being challenged to rethink who we are, and what that means for the next steps we take. One such point is deciding to marry, making a commitment to another person—thereafter we are a wife or husband, and we have a new identity. Another such point is deciding to be ordained, making a commitment not simply to God, but to the church—thereafter we are first a deacon, and then a priest, another new identity.

Who decided that these things should happen? Was it God? Was it the disciple? Maybe those are not the right questions, however. If a vocation is about becoming more authentically who I am in God through following his call, then the decision is surely one taken jointly with God, however consciously I am aware of God's presence at the time. Perhaps the right questions to ask are—does this make me more truly the person God sees, does it give me a space in which I can grow into him?[144] I like the way one person, who was going through the church's discernment process as a prospective MSE, put it: she said it was as if God had said to her "let's do this thing together".

So far, none of this says anything distinctive about people who describe themselves as worker priests or MSEs, whom I describe as PSWs. The individual stories that I have heard from people at all stages of my research are very varied, but there is a consistent pattern in what they say: their sense of vocation is located at least as much (for some, much more) in their secular work as in the church. For one, it was about the "need for ministry in the new parish of the workplace", recognizing that for most of the people he worked with, their home parishes were simply places to sleep. Another had been particularly challenged by the story of Moses, his call in the desert, and the fact that God sent him to God's people because God had heard and seen how they were being exploited by their Egyptian masters. For this PSW, it mattered that he could continue to serve in the area of health and safety in an industry with a history of work-related accidents and illnesses and poor mental health, and of an exploited underclass engaged in casual employment. A third initially thought the right place for her might be the Church Army, or that she might serve as an Evangelist, but advisers in her diocese suggested that MSE might be the way forward, because the nature of her work with victims of abuse meant it was important that she stay in that work. Yet another definitely felt God wanted her to remain in her secular work, because she is almost unique in what she does—as an engineer, she has specific gifts and experience which would not otherwise be available in her industry, and she loves the people she works with. For her, there is a three-fold sense of calling: to her workplace and the people in it, to Eucharistic ministry in a parish, and to people more generally for whom church on a Sunday morning is difficult or impossible (she does a lot of Saturday night shifts).

On the other hand, another person I talked to had engaged with the church's discernment process on and off for a number of years, and at the time of our conversation had decided that for the time being, he was not going to proceed with it. He found that, working on a supermarket checkout, he could exercise a ministry in the conversations he had with shoppers as he scanned their purchases and helped them to pack their bags. Although he felt that he had capacity which could be of benefit to a parish, there was a lack of understanding among vocations advisers he spoke to because he did not fit into their boxes. He intended to continue in his ministry, and see how things developed over time.

To ask "do such people need to be ordained to do what they are doing?" is to ask the wrong question. It is not about whether they need to be ordained in order to be able to do more than they already are, but about the person God wants them to be. To return to the questions posed by the lay reader, quoted in the *Introduction*, who, responding to my *Church Times* letter,[145] asked why the call to serve Christ in the world would require the person to be set apart by all the trappings of priesthood—it is not the call to serve Christ in the world that is the reason why we are ordained, but because the nature of the call Christ gives us is a sacramental one. My interviewees had much to say on this point, and we return to it in Part 2.

CHAPTER 6

The research project

An important way in which human beings develop a sense of their identity is through telling stories, and it is the interviews and conversations with fellow PSWs, plus my own reflections on these stories and my own story, that inform the theology and model of ministry in this book. I did not set out to prove a hypothesis, already identified, but rather to explore with other PSWs how we understand ourselves and the nature of our vocation.

Participants in my research were made aware that their identity might be obvious to anyone who knew their circumstances, as many PSWs occupy unique contexts. I undertook, nevertheless, to do all I could to preserve their anonymity. For that reason, quotations are not attributed to any particular person, and I do not give them names or pseudonyms or describe their particular circumstances.

Research participants

The proportion of SSMs in the Church of England has been fairly steady at just below 30 per cent since 2013. National statistics for 2019[146] (the most recently available at the time of writing) indicate that there were 7,700 stipendiary clergy (excluding ordained chaplains and clergy in non-parish roles) and 2,870 self-supporting clergy in licensed parochial ministry, which includes the sub-categories of NSMs and OLMs,[147] so just over 27 per cent.

In total, over fifty people across both provinces of the Church of England have contributed to my research in the period between 2016 and 2020. Just under thirty were involved at the initial research stage in 2016–17, with six taking part in an in-depth interview process in 2017, and some contributing to a follow-up stage in 2020, together with others recruited through contact with Diocesan Directors of Ordinands (DDOs) and with members of CHRISM. In 2020, I was particularly keen to talk to ordinands and recently ordained PSWs, as well as to talk with as many PSWs as possible about the impact of the COVID-19 pandemic and lockdown on them.

The criteria I used to identify potential participants for my main research project were that:

- they were ordained Church of England priests, who regularly participated in parish ministry;
- they engaged in work which could be reasonably identified as secular for a significant proportion of each week;
- by "secular" work, I meant work which was not directly related to parish ministry or chaplaincy, and which did not require the person to be an ordained, licensed or authorized minister;
- the "work" could be paid, either contracted employment or freelance, or voluntary.

I started my fieldwork in 2016 with a co-operative inquiry group, which consisted of a group of three other PSWs and myself, recruited from an email to SSMs in my diocese. I then used an online questionnaire as a means to access more information about what PSWs were doing, both in the church and outside it, and to recruit people for the subsequent interview stage in 2017. Five of the six interviewees had responded through the online survey; the sixth was a recommendation from someone I met at a conference that summer. The five were selected from those survey respondents who had indicated that they would be willing to be interviewed, in such a way as to provide as wide a range as possible of gender and age, number of years since ordination, and variety of experience in both the institutional church and in secular work.

Throughout my fieldwork, I encountered people who understood their vocation to be what I came to call the PSW. They were working, or had worked, in large, national institutions, in large and small businesses, in the manufacturing industry, and in the charity, education, and service sectors; in conflict mediation and resolution, construction and engineering, counselling and mentoring, education and training, funeral services, information technology, insurance, the NHS, politics (national and local), retail, and social services. They were administrators and bureaucrats, consultants, counsellors, doctors, engineers, entrepreneurs, health and safety officers, lecturers, managers, medical workers, negotiators and mediators (including trades unions), researchers, safeguarding officers, sales staff, teachers, and training officers. Some worked full-time in secular employment; some were retired from paid employment, but were still involved either freelance or with only expenses paid; some worked part-time in secular work and part-time in paid work for the church. Some had only been PSWs, while some had been both full-time stipendiary priests (FTSs) and PSWs at different times; in the final stage of my research, some were ordinands or going through the discernment process.

In the co-operative inquiry group,[148] which kick-started my research, we talked about our life stories—how and why we had reached the point at which we currently found ourselves—and out of that conversation, the two questions which had resonated through my post-ordination journals proved fundamental: "who am I?", "what am I for?" These two questions took us deeper into our personal stories, as we made connections between events in our histories, and our sense of calling to both ordained ministry and our secular work. It became very clear in these sessions that each of us felt we had one vocation, actualised in different ways and contexts, not two (or more). For one of us, priestly ministry preceded secular work by some considerable time, whereas the reverse was true for the others, although seeds of priestly ministry had been discerned much earlier.

In later discussions, we focused on our secular work—what we do, why we do it, how it connects with our ministry. We agreed that all of us were "task driven", that the work mattered for its own sake, and that the need to do it as well as possible was a strong motivator. Towards the end of the first phase of our meetings, the questions that we wanted to answer included: "what is the gift that we bring, that enriches everyone's priesthood?", and "what is our unique gift to the church without which the wider priesthood, and the church, would be impoverished?"

The next stage was the online questionnaire, which I used to get an overall picture of what life was like for PSWs, and to recruit potential interviewees. Themes in the questionnaire responses resonated with those that had emerged in the inquiry group sessions, and proved to be important in the interview data also. It is interesting to note that, although there was considerable variety in the secular and parish contexts of those who responded, there was considerable similarity in the joys and tensions mentioned.

From the responses, it was clear to me that the understanding of vocation—that it is one vocation, not two or more—was a common feature. In some quarters, MSE is known as bi-vocational ministry, but this displays a lack of understanding on the part of some in church leadership, who have not reflected sufficiently deeply on the nature of vocation, as *God's* call to the person, rather than the church's call. All my participants affirmed their clear sense of God's call to them to serve through being a PSW, because their secular work mattered in the establishing of the kingdom: not only was it an important locus and context for their ministry, but the doing of that work was in itself part of what constituted their ministry and discipleship.

Some respondents found joy in being able to integrate completely their faith and working lives, so that they found it hard to untangle what was secular and what was not. Others felt they were both inside and outside the institutional church, and so could, on the one hand, speak prophetically to the church, and, on the other, decode the church for people outside it. Some respondents wrote about linking the church and the world, helping others to meet God where they are, while others emphasized how they would look for God at work in the workplace. Some experienced ordination as permission-giving, enabling them to speak for the church to give it credibility and to challenge perceptions. A few mentioned not having ultimate responsibility for congregations and having the flexibility to respond to people's needs as required. Several commented on how much their secular work and experience contributed to their ministry, and vice versa.

On the other hand, respondents also talked of issues in finding suitable ways to offload, and the lack of understanding shown by FTSs and diocesan personnel. Time was mentioned repeatedly, and in particular the difficulty in balancing commitments, including for families and friends. For some this resulted in their feeling exhausted, torn between competing responsibilities. Isolation was another issue, either because meetings meant to provide support were arranged during the working day, or because FTSs, including incumbents, failed to show understanding of the PSW's situation. Some respondents mentioned being disparaged by FTSs, being treated as an amateur or a "hobby priest", because they were not full-time in the parish.

In response to a question about a typical day, some respondents described days full of activity, both outside the church and inside it, while others described a particular encounter in which they had provided affirmation or a caring, listening ear to someone: "they wouldn't formally ask for an appointment, but seem to clutch at the opportunity to discuss things that are troubling them". One person wrote about taking their skill in sign language (learnt in secular work) into worship; another described how their experience of the church's methods for discerning vocation had been helpful in leading workshops on secular life choices.

A question about a day off was treated with some derision: "a theoretical concept", "a beautiful theory"! Some respondents had found ways to ensure that they enjoyed time relaxing away from their secular work, the parish and chores, but many commented that either there was no day in the week when they were not working, or that, if there were, it would have to be used for housework and shopping. One or two did comment that the balance between their secular work and church ministry was energizing, or that doing all that they did was a choice they made freely, and for one the fact that every day was different helped. One wrote "chocolate in the evening!"

The interview process

Before I started the co-operative inquiry group, I had intended to hold six interviews of an hour to an hour and a half. It became clear, however, that each time the group met, we were able to speak more freely and at greater depth, with increased understanding of each other and of ourselves, than previously. I therefore decided to invite people, through the online questionnaire, for "if appropriate, a morning (or other similar period) in which I can accompany you as you go about your daily life", followed by a recorded interview in the afternoon. This would enable us to go through factual information and to establish a rapport before attempting to reflect at depth on the interviewee's self-understanding and sense of vocation. This day would then be followed by a shorter follow-up interview about a week or ten days later.

It became clear from responses to the questionnaire, however, that this would not work, either because a respondent's secular work involved other people, for whom my presence would be inappropriate, or because they were likely to be sat at a desk in front of a computer. When I negotiated the detail of the interview days with prospective participants, I therefore suggested that I meet them in a place of their choosing for the day: for two of them, that was in their office in their workplace; for the other four, it was their home. We would discuss the participant's context and working life in the morning, and then enjoy a lunch-break when we could simply relax, enjoy one another's company and relate to each other as peers, before the afternoon in-depth recorded interview.

In the recorded interviews, I initiated discussion with two or three pre-selected interesting comments from their questionnaire responses, and then followed that up with anything that had felt particularly significant in the conversations earlier in the day. I then used the same three questions for each interviewee, which I hoped would open up new areas of discussion: "what gets you up in the morning?", "what makes you despair?" and "what are you hungry for?" The final stage of the interview was to ask if there was anything else that the person felt was significant which we had not touched on thus far.

Following each interview day, I wrote up the notes from the morning, and prepared an "I-narrative"[149] of the afternoon's recording. An "I-narrative" includes only those remarks made by the interviewee which start with "I", so not including my contribution to the conversation, and not including anything they said otherwise. The notes and "I-narrative" were sent out to each interviewee in time for them to reflect on them prior to our follow-up conversation. I had trialled this procedure with a friend, who had found that the "I-narrative" worked well as a tool for such reflection, but I did not feel it had further use beyond that, so I was able to assure the interviewees that if they felt it distorted or omitted aspects of what they had said, it would not matter provided they alerted me to that, or to anything they felt I had misunderstood.

The follow-up interviews started with discussion of any corrections that the interviewee wished to make, and anything they wanted removed from the record, or dealt with in very general terms. I then asked them what struck them particularly as they read through the "I-narrative": all said they must have talked about themselves a lot, because there were so many "I"s! I was able to reassure them that not only had I given them only the statements or questions beginning with "I", but I had also invited them to talk about themselves—and indeed, the interview would not have provided what I wanted from it, had that not been the case. What followed then proved the worth of this interview process: the interviewees each identified one or two really significant aspects of our discussions, which we then discussed in greater depth.

Evolution of the research question and a new name

The story of the evolution of my research question is linked to the story of the evolution of the name I eventually decided to use to describe people, who, like me at the time, were licensed priests in ministry in the Church of England, and also engaged in significant secular work. In the Church of England, people who are self-supporting ministers (SSMs) and who see their ministry as primarily focused in their workplaces are known as *ministers in secular employment* (MSEs). In the first year or two of this research project, I realized that, for me at least, it is my being a *priest*, not simply a minister, that is significant, and so I started to use the term *priest in secular employment* (PSE). However, when I wanted to recruit participants for my fieldwork, I used M/PSE, partly as a more inclusive term, and partly because by then I had discovered that at least one of my inquiry group colleagues, an ordained priest, thought of themselves as a minister rather than a priest. During the period when I was working on the analysis of my data, I started to use PSE again; I had discussed with my interviewees whether they felt the designation of "priest" or "minister" was more appropriate, and all agreed that it was "priest". Finally, at a late stage in my analysis, I decided that what the data showed to be significant was not whether or not we are in secular *employment*, but that we do secular *work*, and so the term I finally settled on was *priest in secular work* (PSW), which I now use other than when quoting what people said, or on occasions when it would be obviously anachronistic.

In conversation more recently with someone who self-describes as a worker priest, however, they said that employment matters too, because those who are employed sell their labour for money. This is, of course, true for those who are in contractual employment or who work freelance, but not for those whose work is voluntary. The definition of work I had used throughout my research did not require it to be remunerated, and I did not differentiate between paid and unpaid work. For this reason, perhaps, issues around selling one's labour did not emerge in the inquiry group or in the interviews, and it is not something which I could pursue further.

In the early months of my research, I wrote in my research journal: "What is the ontological secret at the heart of your research? What is at the heart of the research which touches your passionate depths?" and wrestling with these questions has been a key aspect of the development of my research question. Initially, it was all about my struggle to reconcile feelings of joy and fulfilment on the one hand, with confusion, discomfort, disorientation and even hurt, on the other, as I tried to accommodate feeling deskilled, and the blurring of boundaries that derived from my new status as an ordained person in part-time parish ministry continuing to work in mathematics education.

At this stage, my research question was:

> How does an ontological approach to the understanding of the priest in secular employment contribute to a theology of priesthood?

I focused this in two ways:

> What does our identity as priests mean in our secular workplaces and for the work itself?

> What does our identity through our employment in secular work mean for our understanding of ourselves as priests?

This question, with its two sub-questions, emerged from exploring my own experience in the early stages of this research. Other questions that I asked myself during this stage included:

- What am I for?
- How do I integrate my awareness of myself as priest and my awareness of myself in my secular work?

By this point, I had been a PSW for several years, and, gradually finding ways of holding the tension between my priestly and secular identities, was more comfortable with the role. With the inquiry group, I was therefore ready to look beyond my own perspective to consider what the PSW might bring to the institutional church. Reflecting on our initial sessions, I recast my research question in more functional terms:

> The default of priestly ministry as full-time stipendiary ministry is no longer appropriate. How might the model of the M/PSE complement and extend it for the Church of England in the twenty-first century?

The research question continued to evolve as I completed the interview stage of my research, and then met again with the inquiry group to reflect on the interview data. Interesting questions identified at this point included:

- What does it mean to be a minister or priest in a secular workplace?
- How is the ministry of the M/PSE similar to or different from any other priestly ministry, or that of the lay Christian working in a secular job?
- How are we, whose calling it is, to understand the vocation to which God has called us?

As a PSW myself, other questions which I found significant included:

- How am I to get beneath the surface of what we are and do, to explore our self-understanding?
- To what extent is any one of us typical? Are there common threads?
- How do you uncover and process that which it is difficult to know about yourself?

At that final inquiry group session, the form of the research question that we were working on was:

> If the PSE could be considered as a gift of God to the Church of England, how are we, whose calling this is, to understand the vocation to which God has called us?

Subsequent discussion amended this to:

> To what extent and in what ways could the PSE be God's gift to the Church of England in the twenty-first century?

Realizing that "God's gift" was not well-defined, but using the insight this phrase provided, led to a further adaptation:

> What strategic contribution could the concept and practice of the PSE make to ministry in the Church of England?

As I subsequently immersed myself in the main findings and insights from the research, however, it became clear to me that this was not the question I was answering, and indeed that my methodology was not such as to make this a sensible question with which to work.

As a PSW, it matters to me that the general approaches I use in all aspects of my work are consistent, and so, as I wrestled with the form my research question should take, I realized that I could be making better use of insights from my secular work. Following early retirement from contractual employment in 2013, I spent some years as a freelance maths educator (among other things), leading workshops which were data-driven, mainly for teachers' professional development, but sometimes for groups of secondary school students. The workshops started with experiments, which we then discussed in detail to discover what the results were telling us; the next stage was to consider what we would expect to happen, and to make comparisons; the final stage was to use insights from these comparisons to derive the theory that students are expected to know. This did not set out to be a way of introducing students to formal proof, but was a pedagogical approach which prioritized working from data, always asking "what is the story that the data is telling you?" I hoped that this would encourage students to keep open minds, through which understanding and intuition could be nurtured, rather than their simply learning how to manipulate formulae, without any real sense of why they were doing it, or what their results meant. Reflecting on this approach, I concluded that my research also needed to be data-driven, and so I needed to word my question in such a way that I could answer it by writing the story that the data was telling me.

The question I ended up with, therefore, was:

> How do people who are simultaneously ordained, licensed priests in the Church of England, and engaged in secular work, make sense of their particular vocation?

Part 2: The PSW

Curating the voices

In current English usage, a curator is someone who chooses and places works of art or artefacts in a museum, but the word "curator" was originally derived from the Latin *cura*, "to take care". Anyone in ministry in the Church of England will instantly hear cognates of "cure", as in the "cure of souls", and "curate". Originally the curate was the person with whom the bishop shared the cure of souls in a parish; that person is now more generally called the incumbent, who may well have an assistant curate to train or as a colleague. For ten years, I was technically an assistant curate, although in my diocese we are generally referred to as associate priests once we have served our titles as curates. I found it a profoundly moving experience to be given a share in the cure of souls in one of my licensing services,[150] and with this resonance in mind, it pleases me to depict my analysis and interpretation as a form of curation, recognizing that it is important that I "take care" in how I reflect on all my sources, especially the words of the interviewees, and that I "take care" that my presentation of the data enables their authentic voices to be heard.

In an analysis of the process of effective curation, Jonny Baker, whose website describes him as "an advocate for pioneers, lover of all things creative and an explorer of faith in relation to contemporary culture",[151] described an exhibition he had visited in which the use of film and photography created impact through "layered narratives", providing a memorable experience.[152] He wrote that he was greatly affected by it, commenting that it was not "just that I loved some of the works of the artist. It was also the way that the art used the context of the building, and that the journey through the art, while subtle, had a wonderful flow and development to it," which derived from a careful and effective process of curation. A well-curated exhibition is a space for experience, in which people can make connections; it is participative and immersive.

Curation requires selection, so that those exhibits chosen are displayed to good effect, not lost in a morass of detail. It is about providing an opportunity for interaction between the exhibits, their creators, and the audience, while saying something worthwhile about contemporary society.[153] Curating the voices in this research, so that the story of the PSW can be heard loud and clear, required the development of an underlying concept with a narrative flow which would enable different voices to interact to display facets of the identity and vocation of the PSW. I have therefore focused on aspects of participants' experience and their, and my, interpretation of that experience to produce a presentation which is authentic, and allows for diversity, while not attempting to cover all the ground which might be possible.

My research was never intended to be simply an academic exercise: genuine theological reflection arises from engagement, in the presence of God, with issues which are not hypothetical, but arise from situations in which the researcher is personally invested. I decided to start with a framework of questions developed by Jane Leach, which provide a means of naming and exploring issues, listening to and learning from other voices, and so seeking to hear God's voice.[154] Leach's questions focus the researcher's attention on voices that are heard and also those that are absent, including the wider context, the researcher's own voice, the theological tradition and the mission of the church. The voices I listened to included first and foremost my participants, the PSWs who took part in my research, which, together with my own voice, were situated against a background which included scripture and a range of theological literature. The context was an understanding of the church as both the eschatological body of Christ, and a fallen, human institution.

One of Leach's questions also asked whose voices are absent or being silenced. Although my participants frequently referred to FTSs, I have not chosen to give them a voice. Other missing voices include those of my participants' secular work colleagues, and lay Christians engaged in secular work. In part, these omissions stemmed from the need to set realistic boundaries around my research. However, I was also conscious of the need to foreground the voice of the PSW, and not to allow that to be lost or diminished in any way.

The voice of scripture
At a study day in our diocese for licensed ministers, lay and ordained, on St John's Gospel, which I attended at a critical point in my research analysis, the speaker, Professor David Ford, claimed that three questions from the first chapter could provide an interpretive framework for the entire Gospel. I experienced an "aha!" moment, deciding that, whether that is so or not, they would provide a basis for the construction of three theological spaces in which to display facets of the PSW's vocation.

The three questions are:

- "Who are you?" (John 1:19)
- "What do you seek?" (John 1:38)
- "Where are you staying?" (John 1:38)

A method of doing practical theology, known as canonical narrative theology, or "Telling God's Story", provided me with an overall strategy in which these three questions could form a framework.[155] This method originated in the twentieth century in the work of Karl Barth, who went back to the scriptural narrative of Jesus' life to find a way to continue in faith following the horror of the First World War. He found in the Gospels "a narrative that breaks in upon the natural continuum of history and is the basis upon which the events of history are to be judged and interpreted".[156] For Barth, it was not what human beings were doing that was important, but "the doings of God". The theological task is then to work out how our contemporary experience can be interpreted through the lens of the gospel, ensuring that practice is consistent with it.[157] Following Barth, Hans Frei argued "that the scriptural narratives of Jesus contained the key to renewing the Church".[158] He wanted the biblical narrative to be understood *as* narrative, pointing out a fundamental hermeneutic issue: that neither understanding the scriptures as factual and verifiable, nor as unreliable and time-conditioned, is an appropriate way for a Christian to approach them, but that the Bible needs to be understood on its own terms as narrative.[159] His conclusion was that it is necessary to look at the narrative shape of the Gospels as a whole, and not to focus simply on extracts.

This method is not without its critique, however. One strand of criticism derives from a rejection of anything in current society as revelatory of God.[160] Another charges those who, like Frei, developed the method of canonical narrative theology in a way which required the Gospel narratives to be read "realistically", with contributing to a particularly western way of reading scripture, which marginalizes other ways of reading them, such as allegorical, prophetic or mystical readings. Another concern, expressed by Witherington, is that the starting point for use of a biblical extract should be the original meaning of the text so that it is not "abused" through the hermeneutical process.[161]

I hope that my use of the three questions from John 1 does not fall foul of such strictures, as the Gospel narratives are multi-layered, and can sustain many different forms of interpretation. Witherington argued that the purpose of John's Gospel is to present the story of Jesus through the eyes of the Beloved Disciple, creating a "dramatic biography written for Christians to use for evangelistic purposes", so that they could explain "where Jesus came from and where he is going".[162] My use of the three questions is analogous to this, except that where John wanted to explore Jesus' identity, I explore the identity of the PSW. This fits with the strategy of canonical narrative theology, in which scripture provides a key to understanding an aspect of human life. I further believe that God was able to speak in my conversations and interviews with participants, and through my interpretation of the data.

The first question I use is that of the priests and Levites, addressed to John the Baptist: "who are you?" (John 1:19). If the purpose of the Gospel is to present the story of Jesus, then identity is a major focus throughout, starting with this question. Identity is also a major focus for me, in telling the story of the people I have come to call PSWs, and in conceptualizing who they are.

Jesus' first spoken words, as recorded by the evangelist, are: "What do you seek?" (John 1:38). The question resonates for me with what Augustine wrote in his *Confessions*: "The thought of you [God] stirs him [Man, *sic*] so deeply that he cannot be content unless he praises you, because you made us for yourself and our hearts find no peace until they rest in you."[163] Jesus asks his first disciples—and us, his disciples at this time—what they are seeking; the rest of the Gospel shows that the answer is Jesus himself. The question of desire, of wanting to be part of the *missio Dei*, working with God, is part of the story told by PSWs, and so Jesus' question is as pertinent for us as it is for Andrew and his companion.

Responding to Jesus' question, Andrew asked: "Where are you staying?" (John 1:38). The Greek word translated as "staying" is *menein*, with its connotations of abiding and remaining. The particularity of the Gospel is that Jesus lived in a particular place at a particular time; he was a Jew, rooted in his context and culture. As PSWs, we are rooted in an ecclesial context and in our secular work. Part of choosing to be such a person, or feeling that this is who/where we are called to be, is a sense of needing to be a priest in both the church and in the secular world, remaining alongside colleagues for whom the church may well mean nothing at all—and in that place to be a priest.

Locating myself in the curation

As many theologians and others have emphasized over recent years, humans are storytelling creatures, and so to know me "you must know my story, for my story defines who I am. And if *I* want to know *myself*, to gain insight into the meaning of my own life, then I, too, must come to know my own story."[164] I therefore include myself as a voice in the collection I am curating, using words from journals written throughout the period that I was discerning the nature of my vocation. Although I am arguably no longer a PSW, I considered myself to be one until quite recently, because of both my freelance work in maths education and also the work of research and writing, even though the content is theological. For that reason, my location in this research is different from previous research projects I have undertaken. In earlier research in maths education, I wanted to find out about the effectiveness of certain methods of teaching, so my research questions were of the form: how does this particular tool or that medium for teaching or a particular suite of resources contribute to my teaching or that of others, or to student learning? My self-understanding as a teacher and educator was not bound up in these questions, and although I needed to subject my practice to scrutiny, at no point did I feel that I needed to interrogate my sense of who I am. My previous theological research (for my MA dissertation) focused on rural mission, so again was not about my self-understanding.

The process of conducting research in maths education required me to examine my pedagogical biases and assumptions, and on that basis to challenge my practice as a teacher: was what I did consistent with what I believed, and if not, what was I going to do about it? This research project has taken me into many theological areas, making me think deeply about what I take for granted, not just where it affected my own practice as a PSW, but opening up my understanding of what it means to be a priest, what church is, and ultimately, how I meet with and, in so far as I can, understand God.

Throughout the research for my professional doctorate, and as I write this book, I was and am working with my own self-understanding as well as that of my participants. At an early stage, my focus was my own identity, considered through the lenses of priestly ministry in the Church of England, work as a theological category, and exile as a place of not belonging. I wanted to bring these together in a "theology of the 'gap', which is a theology of 'both . . . and'". I identified the "gap" as "the liminal space, which is both threshold and chasm, between church/parish and secular workplace . . . which I, as an MSE and priest, need to inhabit as holy ground, a place where God is at work".[165] That led me into reading about the theology behind the Church of England's understanding of priestly ministry, eventually finding a place where I could situate my own self-understanding as a priest in God the Trinity, rather than specifically in the person of Christ.[166] In formulating the formal research proposal for the professional doctorate, I explained that I wanted "to explore [how] the particularity of the priest in secular employment (PSE) contributes to theologies of priesthood".[167]

During the research, I needed to treat myself as a research subject, interrogating my understanding of myself and my practice, so the personal impact was much greater than in previous research. As an insider, I needed to articulate aspects of my own story which informed how I conducted the research, and why I made the choices I did in method, analysis and interpretation, and in constructing the conceptual framework. At appropriate points I therefore included autobiographical sections as part of the curated material, which form part of this book also, so that those choices are as transparent as possible to the reader.

In reflecting deeply on what my own ordination as priest means to me, and on what the interviewees said about theirs, I still do not see that ordination provides a special status in the way that, for instance, *Lumen gentium* does, when it claims that the "priesthood of the faithful" and "the ministerial or hierarchical priesthood" are different "from one another in essence and not only in degree".[168] My starting point generally is not to accord either priesthood or the church with any special status: priests are human beings, and the church is composed of human beings, and as such priests and church are under both grace and sin. I was a Baptist for many years, and still see the priesthood of all believers as fundamental, with baptism as the calling and ordaining sacrament. However, as one of my interviewees argued, because we are not yet in the fullness of Christ's kingdom, some people are called to be priests in a particular way, to act as signs that nevertheless the kingdom is already among us.

Regarding the church, I see the visible, local church as a potential sign of the kingdom, despite the times in parish ministry when I found myself in despair at some of the outrageous things that were said or done. At such times, I would remind myself that we are all sinners and in need of grace, and that the church, nationally and locally, is no less subject to sinful powers than any other institution. Reading about Augustine's two cities, the *civitas terrena* and the *civitas Dei*, which are inseparable this side of the Parousia (as in the parable of the wheat and the tares, Matthew 13:24–30) gave me a way forward, not simply for the theological background to this work, but as a way of understanding the relationship between the church and the kingdom.

As a Baptist ordinand in the mid 1970s, I had met Paul Fiddes, then a doctoral student, now described in a *Festschrift* in 2014 as "one of the foremost theological thinkers of the modern age".[169] Encountering his and others' work on the Trinity as a perichoretic relationship has been a real gift, not just to my research, but to my faith by providing me with an image which I could link with my work as a maths educator.[170] The analogy of the barn dance, in which people move into a space, then vacate it to allow someone else to move into it, helped me not only to visualize (however imperfectly or inadequately) the relationship that is the Trinity, but also to make connections with the Group Theory that once so delighted me as a maths student, and which line and square dances exemplify. I had always seen maths as saying something significant about God in terms of relationship, pattern and order—concepts which Group Theory develops in a way that satisfied something deep in my soul when I first encountered it.

The voice of the PSW

In order to ensure that I was understanding my interview participants appropriately, during the analysis I sent each of them a very brief summary, which they could redraft if they so wished. Below are the versions we agreed, providing six snapshots of how PSWs understand themselves:

Summary 1: You are someone whose priestly vocation keeps them active in secular life. For you, it is one vocation, to be a priest in whatever context you find yourself, to be aware of God in all of life, and of opportunities to build his *[sic]* kingdom. God's call to you, to be this person, gives you fulfilment and joy.

Summary 2: Your call to priestly ministry arose in your secular workplace, and you always felt that your vocation would keep you on the edge of the church, and the diocesan structures. You feel that your authority as a priest comes from the Trinity, not from the church institution or hierarchy. For you, being ordained priest was a real fulfilment of who you are, a vocation to be worked out through your involvement in education and in the secular world generally, as well as through parish ministry. Being a teacher was also part of who you are, and it mattered to you that you helped your students to achieve as well as they could academically.

Summary 3: You have reflected on what it means to be a priest in secular employment over many years and have compared it with what it means to be a priest in a parish. Being a Christian is about contemplating God, seeing him *[sic]* at work in his world, and making him explicit, not necessarily through words. Being priestly is about facing both ways—towards God and towards the world—and standing with Christ in that place. The PSW is well placed to do this because of their participation in secular work. What matters is not whether we are in secular employment or not, but that we are answering the call of God, who is asking us to be where he needs us.

Summary 4: You reflected on interactions between church and secular, and priesthood and secular work, and how Christians are enabled to live out their faith in their working lives. For you, ordination was what God called you to, but as time went on, you felt that an important part of your vocation was to focus on people at work and a theology of discipleship that embraced this. Your identity is thus to be a priest, but to be a priest who works most of the time in a secular capacity, using your God-given gifts.

Summary 5: For you, it is about blending ministry in church and in school, being grounded in real life, while holding the tensions inherent in having two jobs plus family responsibilities. Although it is not that many years since you were ordained, you cannot now imagine not being ordained, and you take seriously the responsibility this places on you. Your ordination impacted your teaching, but you are finding ways of teaching that are not at odds with your Christian faith and vocation.

Summary 6: For you, it's all about being open to God, 24/7. You are a priest because that's where you can best work for him *[sic]*, both through your Monday–Friday work, and in your parish ministry. Everyone knows you're a priest, and wearing the clerical collar, being identifiable, is part of your evangelism.

CHAPTER 7

Four PSW narratives

In this chapter, I present four narratives which encompass four key relationships for PSWs: with God, with their secular work, with the world, and with the church. These help to illustrate and draw out the summaries in the previous chapter.

The four narratives make substantial use of interviewees' words. Several excerpts, which are particularly rich, are considered in more than one place, so enriching and deepening the description and interpretation of the PSW. At no point is any attribution given: this is to preserve the anonymity of the participants as far as possible. For that same reason, I do not present any case studies, but use words from the interviews to present four composite pictures of the PSW. Where two separate quotations follow each other, they may come from the same person, but equally they may not. Angle brackets < . . . > indicate my part in a conversation, square brackets [. . .] indicate an interpolation. Interpolations do not change the sense of a quotation, but are used to aid clarity.

Narrative 1: What does it mean to be a priest in the secular?

It may not be immediately obvious why one would feel the need to be ordained to then continue working in secular employment, and this came up repeatedly in my conversations with PSWs. Ultimately, as will be seen, this is a question about God's call to the PSW, and about the relationship between the PSW and God, as well as the PSW's relationship with the institutional church.

> I regard ordination rather like the Book of Common Prayer talks about marriage: it's a concession to our sinful natures. We are a priesthood of all believers, but because of our sinful natures we can't do that ultimately collective thing, and we have to have some who are set apart to do it in a very focused way, and in public. But that implies, I think, that all of us have a priestly ministry, not in private, but without the label. And so the thing that's exercised me for a long time is, as I said to you earlier, what does it mean to be a priest in the secular?

The question "why be ordained?" could be construed as a question about why there are priests at all. According to the report *Baptism, Eucharist and Ministry*, the role of the ordained ministry is to "remind the community of the divine initiative, and of the dependence of the Church on Jesus Christ . . . [but] the ordained ministry has no existence apart from the community".[171] For denominations which prioritize the priesthood of all believers, there is very little, if any, ministry which needs to be restricted to ordained priests and cannot be undertaken by any Christian, lay or ordained. In the Church of England, only those who have been ordained priest may consecrate the bread and wine at the Eucharist, and speaking for God by pronouncing absolution and blessing using the pronoun "you" rather than "we" is reserved for the priest.[172] Beyond these requirements of the church, I see nothing special about the PSW compared with a lay Christian active in the world—both PSWs and lay Christians are part of the *missio Dei*.[173] Since this research is about the self-understanding of PSWs, an exploration of why PSWs are priests is required, recognizing that the very fact of preparing for ordination, and then exercising priestly ministry, necessarily impacts the PSW's understanding of, and construction of, their identity.

"Why are you ordained?" is often interpreted as a question about being and doing, ontology and function. As one interviewee put it:

> I . . . knew a curate . . . who used to say, "Why do you have to be a priest to do your work?" to which I answered, "I don't have to be a priest, but I am, and what makes you ask about having to be?"

At another point in his interview, he wondered "why anyone would want to distinguish between ontology and function", assessing this as "nonsense" because "doing and being are two sides of the same coin, though being the more fundamental". The ordination service does not involve magic, but the process which leads up to it, and the sense that something really significant is happening at the service, contributed to my participants believing that their priestly ordination was ontological, not simply functional: that because of it, they had a priestly identity that they had not had before. In taking up the functions of a priest, self-understanding and sense of identity are inevitably changed. The question, "what does it mean to be a priest in the secular?", is thus about identity, more particularly priestly identity and vocation, and also about what we mean by "secular".

My own vocation to be a PSW emerged through my struggle with the demands of parish ministry and my secular work, a struggle which ultimately became the means through which I realized that this is the life I have been given, with all its complexity and tensions, in which I am called to be both a Christian and a priest. Others found it easier to understand the nature of their vocation, although understanding quite what it meant was not necessarily obvious: "The thing I loved about MSE was having to make sense of it as a Christian vocation . . . in settings that were non-religious, by and large." This interviewee had come to believe that his vocation was to be a Christian in a secular workplace; he went into that workplace, however, already an ordained priest with several years' experience of parish ministry. For other PSWs, it is a conscious choice or calling right from the start of their ministry: "I already felt called to carry on working . . . and for that to be the main focus of my ministry."

All the interviewees made it very clear that their vocation to be a priest does not reside only in the service they offer to the church, but is about "being a priest all the time . . . I do all this and I am a priest, they're all just inextricably linked together". The secular is brought into the church, and *vice versa*: "You are very much a two-way . . . things go both ways":

> ... it's about living in the theological interim between Pentecost and the Parousia. We live with the grace of the Holy Spirit, and we live with the persistence of sin ...

> ... It's actually about living in that ambiguity that's at the heart of what living as a Christian is about ...

For one interviewee, this meant understanding the political arena as "exactly where Christians should be", because her "calling is to stay stuck in ... God in the mass on Sunday, God in the mess on Monday". She continued that a great deal of what being an MSE is about is "trying ... to get rid of those boxes", one box labelled "church" and a separate box labelled "real life".

The vocation to be a priest in the secular means that the PSW is publicly identified not only as a Christian, but as a representative of the church: "It's about being seen as a person who is the church throughout the week, rather than ... just somewhere where you go on a Sunday." In representing the church, the PSW is "better placed to then enable other people ... to work it out for themselves", not least because they have had to work out for themselves what it means to be a Christian in the secular. Being a public representative of the church has its difficulties, however, and all the interviewees were clear that part of their calling was to be someone who could and would represent a Christian perspective in their workplace, whether or not this set them at odds with management or their colleagues on occasion.

Given that anyone can exercise a ministry which could be characterized as "priestly" in nature in their workplace, I asked all the interviewees why they had felt they needed to be ordained. All agreed that the fact of ordination did make a difference for them: "I think that being a priest teacher, or teacher priest, whichever way you want to play it, is who I am; and I particularly feel that this is a role that I was born to play." Another said: "It's a good question ... I never felt that I had a satisfactory answer ... ", but since retiring from much of her secular work, she felt that she was beginning to get a better grasp of why it had mattered that, when she was ordained, she continued in that work. She could not explain it in the form of a logical argument, but instead told me how she had acted in a priestly way with a colleague, who with his wife had decided to abort a baby likely to be born with Down's syndrome. She felt that she had helped the colleague to begin the process of forgiving himself, because she was able to offer absolution, although not naming it as such. Any Christian could do this, but a priest, who has had to think deeply about what it means to absolve people in God's name, is perhaps better placed to do it: "I think what it [ordination] gave me was a confidence that I could speak with authority... that I had God, the Trinity, behind me and within me, when I was operating."

All the PSWs I interviewed found that their secular work, workplaces and colleagues, contributed quite as much to their parish ministry, as their involvement in the parish contributed to their secular lives:

> ... [the] job ... here is so important, that it sustains a huge amount of my energy for doing the parish work. And I think I've got a balance at present, where the two really feed off each other in a positive [way], rather than detract from each other.

Summarizing, being a priest in the secular means being "church for them their way", taking church out of the religious frame and into the secular, and enabling a Christian narrative to have some credibility outside the church. It is not two vocations, one to ministry and one to secular work, but one:

> ... because I'm one person and I am a priest. Whatever I'm doing it's as a priest, even if it's not obviously priestly and I'm not wearing robes or a collar, I am a priest in whatever I do and I'm mindful of that wherever I am.

> ... you are not simply a priest in certain places or in particular contexts, you're a priest all the time. ... it's not a priest *and* do all that, it's I do all this *because* I'm a priest. ... It's about the whole of your life is your service to God; the whole of your life is your vocation, whatever you happen to be doing. [original verbal emphases]

Narrative 2: Does it make any difference to how we do our jobs?

In teasing out what it means to be a PSW, a key question is whether and how it affects the way we do our secular work, and whether and how it affects our relationships with secular colleagues.

> ... it's who I am, and it comes back to this ontological question: this is what I gave myself to be. ... I was priested, and I can't erase that from my character, if I can put it like that. ... it's ... what are you at the bottom? ... But the fascinating question for me, which I've asked often, is—does it affect the way I do my job here? And I don't know the answer to that ...

During the course of the informal contextual conversations that started each interview day, the interviewees told me about their secular jobs, and how their priestly ordination fitted into the picture, and we discussed the impact of each on the other. While I did not specifically ask the question "does it [ordination] make any difference to how we do our jobs?", I did probe connections they saw between their work in the church and their work in their secular workplaces. Some interviewees felt that it was entirely positive, that each fed off the other constructively: "My calling is to be blended between ministry in secular employment ... Ministry in the day job ... and ministry in the parish ... are equal and complementary to me". For others it was less clear: saying that ordination does make a difference could be construed as disparaging how colleagues do their jobs, while saying that there is no difference would suggest that ordination, or even faith, is meaningless in the workplace:

> But does your faith matter to you in the place of work? Well, yes, actually, it really does, it really needs to. So are you better at it than your secular colleagues? No, it would be wrong to say that I was, and that would be an awful thing to say. So I'm strung there between two different perceptions, looking with two eyes: one which I'm saying it's very important, my faith; and the other in which I'm saying it doesn't make me a better employee.

For some interviewees, the main issue was the practical one of keeping two significant areas of work going, while doing both properly:

> ... although I've got much better at saying, no—I can't do that here, and I need to do that there.... it's easy to feel a jack of all trades and master of none, that you do two half jobs badly, rather than the one job well.

This echoes a concern that some of the 1970s NSMs expressed in the 1983 report, that it was important to do their secular work properly, and not to allow ministry to detract from that.[174] Being in a secular workplace, allowing the challenges to be part of our priestly formation and ministry, however, is at the heart of being a PSW. The PSW has to:

> ... do a decent job of whatever it is you're being paid for, and then, okay, the other, if appropriate, will come. But you cannot expect to go in there as the great "I am" now that I've got this collar, and all the rest of it, and have people treat you in any sort of different way ...

That means sharing in everything, being as involved as everyone else in all that happens, good or bad:

> ... one of the things I enjoyed about the [workplace], was working with the tough bits because that way we were working with the real, and, in some sense, that we can't be so precious about our place, that we have always to be pure ... [we have to] be happy to get our hands dirty, or else who will?

While PSWs who work in the construction or manufacturing industries, for instance, or in the health service, may literally get their hands dirty at work, none are immune from issues at work which challenge their faith, and "getting our hands dirty" then has a personal cost. A teacher talked about the effect on her school of suddenly being classed as "failing" when the criteria changed: "The stress that that immediately almost overnight brought to everyone at school, was horrendous," leading to:

> ... some really unfortunate patterns of behaviours, which I found very uncomfortable and stressful. Sometimes I was a victim, sometimes I was just a witness. ... I tried during that time to talk about it [to those in the church who should be able to offer support to a priest], but there was just total incomprehension of what it's like to go to the same people, the same place of work day after day after day, when you're being reduced in the national press ...

She talked later about the "corruption" this situation had led to in school, as people resorted to inappropriate ways to improve results, and the way that affected her as a priest.

For one interviewee, there had been a moral cost in working in a service which was understaffed, relative to the demand: "Either we can help nobody ... or we could help some people, but we had to make the judgement." Another talked about conducting disciplinary hearings, a part of her current working life that she did not enjoy, while for another it was about working out how to teach business studies given the assumption that profit is the driving force in business, which he found increasingly uncomfortable. One interviewee told me about a female PSW he had known who worked as a secretary in a small building firm, whose experience was very different from his in a professional workplace:

> ... I learnt from her about what I didn't know about, because of the nature of the life of the whole of that firm. And the whole question of what is divine was very different for her and for them ...

An interviewee who worked in manufacturing industry emphasized the importance of putting on his high-visibility jacket and hard hat, experiencing all that his colleagues experienced. I doubt that he would, as I foolishly did in an interview with a recently retired manager, suggest there might be a compassionate way to make people redundant. The PSW to whom I said this firmly rejected it: "There is nothing vaguely ... kind or affirming about being made redundant," but she completely accepted that, as part of her role, it was necessary for her to be involved. Rather than feeling that, as a priest, she should keep clear of such situations, she ensured that she did it in a way which prioritized the welfare of the employee. She later commented that when she occasionally meets worker priests, who fulfil their priestly vocations through working on the shop floor, she defends her way of being a worker priest because management is also work that needs the impact of priestly presence.

Most PSWs, while perhaps not literally getting their hands dirty, use this as a metaphor to express how our way of being priests is different from that of many FTSs:

> ... people who have spent most of their life in full-time parish-based ministry, simply don't have the same experiences ... I mean, all this management stuff and money, and decisions, and risk-taking and so on, and ... that's not what you're about if you're a member of the clergy.

A PSW who had started out as an FTS talked about the "alienation of work" that he had observed among people in his parish who worked in a government weapons research station. He had wanted one to be a churchwarden, but this person felt he could not be confirmed, and so could not be a churchwarden, because being confirmed would force him to confront moral questions he felt he could not afford to face if he wanted to keep his job.

Anecdotes like this contributed to my interpretation of the PSW as necessary to the church's involvement in the world in the *saeculum*, witnessing as it does to the need for Christians to live out their faith in "Babylon" Both the PSW interviewees who had started out as FTSs found that it was the "work questions people were bringing into their engagement with church, [that] we didn't know how to deal with", which ultimately led them out of full-time parish ministry to become PSWs, seeing it as important for the church that some priests grapple with such issues. Indeed, one commented:

> ... an otherwise admirable bishop ... would say ... "what can I do for you?" And yet, I think we all felt it was the wrong way around: what could we do for him? Because, in a way, what an

> MSE does is to bring ... an experience of work into the life of the clergy.

The alienation of work is an aspect of the *civitas terrena*, of life in Babylon. One could interpret the situation in which the putative churchwarden found himself as an instance of "Bonhoeffer's dilemma", where a Christian feels that there is no choice but to be tainted by evil. Bonhoeffer wrote that "I should like to learn to have faith. ... I thought I could acquire faith by trying to live a holy life ... I discovered later ... that it is only by living completely in this world that one learns to have faith. ... By this-worldliness I mean living unreservedly in life's duties, problems, successes and failures, experiences and perplexities."[175] This was written in a letter dated 21 July 1944. On 20 July 1944, an unsuccessful attempt had been made to assassinate Hitler, and papers were subsequently found, linking Bonhoeffer to the conspiracy; he was also convicted of helping Jews to escape Germany. As a result, he was hanged on 9 April 1945. Bonhoeffer never attempted to justify his involvement in the war, which was clearly at odds with his pacifism, but took responsibility for it: "Only at the cost of self-deception can he [the person who would be virtuous] keep himself *[sic]* pure from the contamination arising from responsible action. ... Who stands fast? Only the man whose final standard is not his reason, his principles, his conscience, his freedom, or his virtue, but who is ready to sacrifice all this when he is called to obedient and responsible action in faith and in exclusive allegiance to God—the responsible man, who tries to make his whole life an answer to the question and call of God."[176]

This could stand as a summary for how PSWs understand their vocation, although few would expect to find themselves in such extreme circumstances as Bonhoeffer. The PSWs saw it as important that not only would they seek the welfare of the people they work with (cf. Jeremiah 29:4–9), but that they were implicated in the same ethical issues as their fellow workers, and so could present an authentic Christian response. One interviewee told me about asking a work colleague, who was not a person of faith, for a reference. His colleague agreed, saying that:

> ... if more priests were like X [the PSW], I might actually consider, because X talks with me, listens to me, respects me,

he does a job of work and I can relate to all that he says. If more people were like X in the church, I would actually look again.[177]

The PSWs I spoke to were clear that they were not there to be workplace chaplains, apart from the two for whom it was part of their role description, with some of their working time specifically allocated for it. Even these two differentiated between that part of their work and their other responsibilities. A key difference is that, because the PSW is paid to do a secular job, they are subject to the same pressures as everyone else, whereas:

> . . . the chaplain comes in and goes away, and comes in and goes away, and is insulated, in a personal sense, from what the people to whom they are chaplain are experiencing, because they don't experience it themselves.

The PSW stands anxiously with the other employees when redundancy, or pension rights, are discussed, not arriving after the axe has fallen to provide pastoral support for those affected. In a secular workplace, you earn any right you may have to speak of matters of faith by being a fellow worker, taking your job seriously, doing it as well as you can, and taking what comes, good or bad, alongside everyone else.

Does our priesthood make a difference to our secular work? Work matters for the PSW not just because it helps us to identify with, and be accepted by, our colleagues, and not just because it gives us credibility, because we are subject to the same pressures and issues as they are. All the interviewees saw their secular work as an end in itself, and not a means to something else. They all talked about the fulfilment and satisfaction it gave them: "Your work is valuable to God." Being good at our jobs, doing them well, is as much a part of the PSW's service to God, our way of participating in the *missio Dei*, as anything we do in church or in the parish. One interviewee told me of an occasion when his line manager complimented him on being his best bureaucrat: "I know . . . you didn't accept the call to be a priest in the Church of God to be a bureaucrat, but it doesn't stop you being good at it." A PSW, who had recently retired as a school teacher, commented that "the world of education hasn't let me go yet, and I'm not letting it go", because she felt she still had something to offer there. Both were celebrating their ability to do their secular work well, because they felt it was important to God, as did the PSW now working in a portfolio of voluntary occupations, one of which is research in a very niche area, which she saw as "exploring the real meaning of what some people a long while ago did . . . partly for the glory of God". As she said this, I remembered a girl I sat next to in school, many decades ago, who used to write AMDG in the top margin on every page of her exercise books—*Ad Maiorem Dei Gloriam*, to the greater glory of God.

For me, this sums up a major feature of the vocation to be a PSW, that our secular work is in many ways the key to our priestly vocation: we do it as well as we can to the glory of God, to help build Christ's kingdom here on earth, to participate in the *missio Dei*:

> . . . your work is valuable to God, it's just everything you do. . . . because it's your job, that's your vocation.
> <And you do it well because you—this is what you do and that's important to God?>
> Yes.

Narrative 3: How does this proclaim Christ to the world?

This narrative is about the relationship between the PSW and the wider, secular world.

> . . . that's the acid test for anything we do here, how does this proclaim Christ to the world? . . . proclamation isn't just shouting; proclamation is saying, actually, there's a whole way of looking at life if you factor in even covertly the God of Jesus Christ. And factor that in and the world looks different, and you may even concede it looks better. Even if you don't accept the gospel of Christ, you may concede that this is a way of looking at life that answers questions that your world view doesn't answer.

The PSW who works alongside others may well have far more opportunity to demonstrate a different way of looking at the world than does the FTS who only sees people in the time outside work: "I think it's a question of being a presence, of bringing the church into the community in a very tangible way." An important aspect of being a PSW in a secular workplace, therefore, is the opportunities this creates to form connections and bridges between life in the church and life outside it. The PSW, in common with lay Christians in the workplace, has the duty and the opportunity, as part of their contribution to the *missio Dei*, to ensure that a Christian perspective is heard, which expresses "how religious people think, rather than what people think religious people think", and which helps people to see the world differently.

The interviewees understood proclaiming Christ as something that happens through relationships, and that it is generally "slow and long and gentle". For one, it is about enabling others to understand their Monday to Saturday lives as part of the *missio Dei*:

> ... it's about ordinary people being able to see and feel that everything that they do is part of vocation, in inverted commas, or building the kingdom, or service to God, or whatever particular terms you want to use for it.

She illustrated what she meant by talking about the "lady who does the coffee rota" who is a hairdresser, listening to her clients' problems, giving advice, chatting to them, and generally making them feel better about themselves and their lives. It is not uncommon for lay Christians to feel that it is running the church coffee rota which forms their Christian service, rather than understanding their daily work as part of the *missio Dei*. It is part of the role of the PSW to help such a person recognize that what she is doing in her daily work is Christian service, because the PSW has "to work it out for themselves, [so] they are better placed ... to help people work it out for themselves", especially if the "vicar is not going to acknowledge that [e.g. hairdressing] as a form of service, as a general rule". Failure to understand that secular work contributes to the *missio Dei* is common to both ministers and lay Christians, and indicates that, whatever they may say, they actually believe that the kingdom of God is somehow more present in the visible church than outside it. Because many Christians limit their understanding of ministry to what happens in church, part of the significance of PSWs is that their ministry "is not merely non-stipendiary, it's secular".

A PSW employed in a very diverse workplace, where there are people of all faiths and none, saw no problem in talking about matters of faith with them all, not to convert others to his way of thinking, "but trying to broaden the horizons and the world view of those around me, but also accepting and listening to them with their faith". His openness to insights from the faith of others resonates with the interviewee who admitted that there are times when his Christian world view "doesn't answer the questions that their world view does". All the interviewees indicated in one way or another that just because we are people of faith, it does not mean *we* have all the answers (only God has those), and that we should be prepared to learn from our non-religious colleagues and colleagues of other faiths.

Not all PSWs are in a working context where it is appropriate to speak openly about their faith, however. One interviewee talked about times in his secular work as a counsellor when he felt he "was making God explicit within the situation, without necessarily the other person in the situation having any grasp of what I was thinking or pointing to". When I pressed him on this—how could he make God explicit if he was the only person who was aware of God in the situation?—he responded that he "could make God explicit by making the love of God . . . more explicit to that person, without it being obvious to that person that we're actually talking about the divine *per se*". This was also illustrated by another interviewee, describing an act of remembrance which she had led for a work colleague who was killed. It was not a Christian service, but she created "a space where what you would perceive to be the right values, or even the virtues of Christianity can thrive" without being overtly labelled as such:

> . . . it was . . . clear from the things that people said during that act of remembrance, that several of them, although it was explicitly not religious, were interpreting it, in effect, as a religious activity for them, for them personally.

In opening up a space for all, whether of faith or not, she too was making God explicit for those who chose to be aware of God's presence, while observing the constraints of a secular workplace.

Not surprisingly, interviewees referred to some of Jesus' parables, where the presence of the kingdom is likened to a light on a hill, to salt, and to yeast (Matthew 5:13–15; 13:33), but the most common analogy they used was that of a bridge, connecting the world of the church to the world that most people live in most of the time:

> I think that MSEs . . . are incredibly important in terms of building that bridge, and meeting people where they're at, which is not ten o'clock on a Sunday morning for an hour. . . . they wouldn't dream of knocking on their parish priest's door; they probably don't even know where the parish priest lives, or where the church is . . . But they'd be very happy to talk to me about something that's quite a deep issue of faith, and I think that's where the real salt and light is, actually, that we're going out to people and meeting them in their day-to-day life.

Another interviewee claimed that "the ordinary world is now so evacuated of theological concepts, in any overt sense . . . it needs an act of translation". The bridge is two-way, however, because not only does the secular world not recognize the language or concepts of the church, the church often fails to see what is theological outside its own parameters. One interviewee illustrated this by describing an encounter between the church and industry in Sheffield in the post-war years:

> . . . radicalizing the church by its encounter with the secular . . . failed, because the missioners discovered, they believed, the Holy Spirit hard at work in the steelworks, but they couldn't find a language that would bridge the gap. If they talked about what they found, the church said, "What's interesting about that? What's theological about that?" If they talked about it in theological language, the steelworkers said "bollocks"!

He then lamented that such encounters proved to be "a dead end", and so "that's why I do the job I do, partly", seeing the constant need to translate not simply between the church and the secular world, but also between the theologians and the "ordinary Christian", helping them to understand "this is why this matters to your life". The "constant translation and iteration of theological language and secular language" is "at the core of being a priest". When I suggested it was about being bilingual, he said it was more like moving from Pidgin to Creole, because Creole is "a more worked out language", but it can be understood by Pidgin speakers and by people who speak the language from which Pidgin and Creole are derived, even though all of them may only be fluent in one form of the language.

Another interviewee reflected on how her theological training helped her to interpret what was going on in her secular workplace:

> There's no way I talk about redemption, there's no way I talk about absolution, but if you found a problem and a number of people have worked together, and we've sorted it out and things are better afterwards, then you can sit down and work out how that happened and what you did, and how we've improved. And I may go away and think to myself, well, that's a very good example of redemption, absolution . . .

Bridging the gap "is [also] about . . . bringing secular things into church, or into prayer":

> . . . when people talk to me, I am praying as they talk, asking God to tell me what to say or whether I need to be quiet. . . . I am always in prayer, asking that God guide me in what to say, rather than me just firing off.

Another interviewee, remembering someone he had worked with many years ago, who was a Methodist lay preacher, talked of the sense of compassion and prayer that this person brought into the workplace: "It's something of the presence of God . . . a sense that the contemplation of God at some level, produces or substantially upholds that level of compassion." For him, our calling is "to contemplate the whole of life and look for God", recognizing that "the secular world … teaches you some ways of looking for God". In a wonderful conclusion, he summarized how we make God known in the world:

> I have an image of myself about one of the gifts of God, if one is a believer, which is that he requires us to write our lives across the sky. By which I think I mean that why or what we do may be of little worth in some ways, and we shouldn't insist that it's different from that. Nevertheless, it's as though it is of huge worth …

PSWs are called to write their lives across the sky, not instead of others, but as public Christians, representing the church, proclaiming Christ to the world, and so participating in the *missio Dei*.

Narrative 4: What is the role of the PSW in the life of the church?

> … it's a wonderful role if you're the right person. If you don't mind being outside the city gates, or just standing on the thresholds with your head swivelling both ways in and out. And if you don't mind that the hierarchy of the diocese has all come through stipendiary ministry, usually the large churches, usually theological colleges, and they don't really get where you're at.

In my conversations with PSWs, the relationship between the PSW and the institutional church came up frequently, often as a way of expressing tensions or negative feelings. For one interviewee, talking of her retirement from full-time paid employment: "My vicar did think … that he was going to get a curate … And I'm afraid I've been a bitter disappointment to him from that point of view." The theological underpinning for understanding one's priesthood does not suddenly change overnight: once a PSW, always a PSW, perhaps.

There was ambivalence about the concept of parish itself for some:

> I love the parishes, and I love the fact that every single person living in this country has a parish priest. Now, I wouldn't want to go against that at all, but it may have reflected a medieval way of life, but it doesn't reflect a current way of life.

For at least one of the interviewees, there was no ambivalence—for him, the parish system is irrelevant:

> I have always thought outside of the parish boundaries—to me, parish boundaries don't exist. They didn't exist for Christ, they didn't exist for his apostles—and it's outreach to whoever, whenever, however.

Others did not question the existence of the parish system, but did question how the PSW is perceived by the institutional church: "There's little understanding of how we are building the church here, rather than in the parish." A critique of the institutional church, voiced in different ways by all the interviewees, was that it does not understand that there is a way of participating in the *missio Dei*, which is not about being in church on a Sunday or doing church-based activities. If the PSW is only valued for what they do in church, it can appear that our role is simply to "prop up the parish system on a Sunday morning" without there needing to be "any more money, because there isn't any".

This feeds into a stereotype of the PSW that they are "amateurs, or they're the hobby priests". One interviewee felt that FTSs view him as:

> ... playing at it a bit ... I got into quite a difficult argument with somebody once about this, about having to—it was almost you work eight days a week, you're lucky; I work fifteen days a week for no pay! And it almost got to that, and we both ended up being absurd parodies of ourselves, I'm sure.[178]

Another interviewee claimed that:

> I think that there's still a huge perception amongst clergy who've gone through—certainly those who've gone through the

traditional route of away to college for three years and so on, that we as SSMs are playing at it a bit, and we're not valued, or we didn't ought to be valued as highly as others.

Although it is the PSW's failure to spend all their time in parish-related ministry that incurs such comments, money also comes into it, although as "MSE is not merely non-stipendiary, it's secular", that is to miss the way in which PSWs contribute to the *missio Dei*. Money may well decide things in the end, however, because as one interviewee observed, we "SSMs will become the default model anyway", since there are not enough people being ordained as FTSs, and the church "couldn't afford to pay". However, for the time being, it remains the case that the "bulk of the Church of England organizationally exists on people who are either stipendiary, or who are working on a voluntary basis a sort of stipendiary pattern".

Overall, there was a general feeling amongst the interviewees that although the institutional church needs its PSWs, it simply does not grasp that our ministry beyond the church is part of the *missio Dei*, and that it has little interest in finding out: "The hierarchy of the church . . . [is] . . . benevolent at a distance, but not involved, not interested and not really understanding." However, this interviewee later noted that this lack of interest does at least give her "the freedom to just get on with it"! It is not that the church does not want to support its PSWs, more that:

> . . . none of the support that's offered appears to be the right support . . . is it that those trying to respond are so trammelled by the way the church does things, that it can't actually equip people for a very "unchurch-y" context?

The interviewees all observed that generally their secular colleagues were much more likely to take an interest in their ministry and church work than their parish colleagues were to take an interest in their secular work: "My secular colleagues have always found it very much easier to—from their point of view—to understand what I'm doing, than my church colleagues, my ordained colleagues." Another, talking of the support he receives from other staff at his school, said: "It's nice, the recognition of the head, and, indeed, a lot of the staff . . . I feel very valued in all that I do by a lot of staff." All the interviewees commented on their perception that the institution of the church sees one normative way of being a priest, but that being a PSW is quite different: "I think it's partly because people who have spent most of their life in full-time parish-based ministry simply don't have the same experiences", and "there is so much in stipendiary ministry that is both busy and really rather ecclesiastical".

One interviewee, however, remarked:

> I think it's difficult to know where—it's really difficult to know where this comes from. I think there's a genuine fear, in some cases, that we may look horribly much more competent at certain things than they are. . . . I think there is certainly a residual fear from stipendiaries of SSM clergy, who, in many cases, appear to be having it all. They've got the job; they've got the money; they've got all sorts of things . . .

For her, those who refer to priests who are not full-time as "amateurs or . . . hobby priests" do so from fear and envy of the "other" who appears to be doing so much better.

She was not alone in highlighting the issue of competence. Another interviewee commented: "They don't have the skillset to relate to the world around them." As one interviewee observed, however: "It's not quite what they think, is it?" For both PSWs and FTSs observing the other, the perception may well be but a faint shadow of the reality. Nevertheless, the lack of interest in PSWs' secular work means that skills and leadership qualities gained in the secular workplace are frequently simply ignored in the church. When I observed that this is a waste, the interviewee I was speaking to responded: "It really is, and an exploitation of our loyalty and commitment, and faithfulness." For now, the church is:

> . . . just hoping that people such as us will keep doing what is already there . . . if we don't rock the boat, but, yes, all these professionals out there as MSEs with all those leadership qualities, but not regarded within the church structures as leaders . . .

It is perhaps not surprising that the institutional church has difficulty in knowing how to recognize the ministry that the PSW provides outside parish and diocesan structures. Priests require a licence to minister in a parish, or at least "permission to officiate", which works well for those whose ministry is all parish (or diocese) based, but more problematic for those PSWs who see their secular workplaces as the primary locus of their ministry. The result is that "the church is often puzzled . . . as to whether they can license people to ministry in the secular workplace". Illustrating this issue, one of the interviewees talked about someone he had known, who was classed as a "work-based non-stipendiary" by his diocese. He was employed by the Bank of England, and initially licensed as a priest to both a parish and to the Bank (although only the Bank contributed to his salary): "And it worked well, until his line manager changed and would have nothing to do with it. And so it was the wrong model . . .".

—

The next three chapters take the three questions from the first chapter of John's Gospel—Who are you?, What do you seek?, and Where are you staying?—and use them to go deeper into some of the themes that have been mentioned or hinted at in the four narratives.

CHAPTER 8

Who are you?

> ... when the Jews sent priests and Levites from Jerusalem to ask him [John the Baptist], "Who are you?" He confessed and did not deny it, but confessed, "I am not the Messiah." And they asked him, "What then? Are you Elijah?" He said, "I am not." "Are you the prophet?" He answered, "No." Then they said to him, "Who are you? Let us have an answer for those who sent us. What do you say about yourself?"
>
> *John 1:19–22*

A new phenomenon had arisen out in the wilderness, not under the auspices of the priests and Levites, who therefore wanted an explanation. In this passage, we hear the representatives of the established religious authority of the time questioning John the Baptist about his credentials. In John's Gospel, the function of John the Baptist is not so much to be the forerunner who prepares the way (e.g. Mark 1:1–8), as to be the first person to identify Jesus as the Messiah (John 1:29–34). This necessitated ensuring that people understood that he himself was not the Messiah, but that his role was that of a witness. All Christians are similarly called to be witnesses, to point to Christ in our midst (e.g. Acts 1:8; 1 Peter 3:15; Romans 10:14–15). Part of the role of the PSW is to be such a witness, and that is perhaps the short answer to "who are you?"—but it does not give any indication as to what is distinctive about the PSW.

Theological background to "identity"

"I define who I am by defining where I speak from . . . in social space, in the geography of social statuses and functions . . . and also crucially in the space of moral and spiritual orientation within which my most important defining relations are lived out": that was the claim of the Canadian philosopher Charles Taylor in his 1989 book on identity in the modern age.[179] At the end of the first session of my co-operative inquiry group, we agreed to focus on the questions: "Who am I?" and "What am I for?" At the following session, as each participant took it in turn to answer those questions, we explored together our self-understanding as PSWs. In our final session, after the interviews were completed, when we reviewed the data from them, we commented on the richness of the interviewees' stories, and our sense that we had been privileged to hear previously unheard, even untold, stories.

Stories such as those the interviewees told form "living human documents", which are "authentic accounts of lived experience presented in a form that can be read and analysed". Such documents "are always dialogical", because they "witness to . . . conversational encounters with other people, other world views and with God", in which "self and identity are . . . formed through interaction with others".[180]

Narrative construction of identity

It is impossible to overestimate the significance of the stories we tell ourselves and others in establishing our sense of who we are—our identity—and reading through the interview transcripts, I was constantly aware of their narrative form. In the interviews, as we explored what it means to be a PSW, participants told stories about their lives and about their encounters with God and with others, which helped them to make sense of themselves; when they struggled to make a point, they would tell a story to exemplify what they were trying to say. There was a holding together of memory, anticipation and present experience,[181] which supports Ganzevoort's claim that a narrative perspective can be traced, even when the form of a text is not obviously that of a narrative.[182]

In a seminal essay, Crites claimed that the stories we tell express our culture. He designated the implicit stories which form our sense of who we are, and which are also formative for our culture, as "sacred": "not so much because gods are commonly celebrated in them, but because men's [sic] sense of self and world is created through them".[183] He further argued that "every sacred story is a creation story", not just because a self is created in it, but because "the story itself creates a world of consciousness and the self that is oriented to it". It is through story that we can hold together past, present and future, because narrative is the only form in which "the full temporality of experience" can be unified, holding together what is remembered, what is anticipated and what is experienced.[184]

Ganzevoort argued that identity is "not some essential quality that needs to be uncovered, but the story one tells about oneself for a particular audience".[185] It is through telling and retelling our stories that we create for ourselves our sense of who we are: we construct a reality, which we then endow with objective meaning, while still allowing further reconstruction. Even when the form is not obviously that of a narrative, there can be a narrative perspective in which "the construction of meaning and thus also the construction of religious meaning . . . take place in the encounter between the human mind and an external reality". The form that such meaning takes is narrative, because "we experience life in story-like forms . . . We live our lives from day to day, but we understand our life as if it were a story".[186]

Ganzevoort developed a narrative hermeneutic,[187] which weaves together two three-fold frameworks: a temporal framework of past, present and future,[188] and a contextual framework of narrator, text (understood as action as well as words) and audience.[189] Both were in evidence in the co-operative inquiry group: as we talked, we told our stories (narrator and audience), often responding to each other with a further story, bringing our life-histories into the mix (past, text), our present contexts, and our hopes and fears for the future. In the interviews, the overall direction of the conversation was decided by me, but I remained alert to signals from the interviewee that they wanted to head off in a different direction because that is where their telling of their story was taking them at that moment. When I felt it appropriate, I contributed my own stories, sometimes as a way of empathizing, sometimes to suggest a different interpretation for us to consider. Looking back at the data,

I see the temporal and contextual three-fold frameworks being woven seamlessly together time and time again.

Arguing that identity is not absolute, the theologian Elaine Graham claimed that our identities are formed in the culture we inhabit and in which we perform our selves.[190] Discussing whether identity is discovered or constructed, Appiah rejected such dichotomies, claiming that because we are not impotent in shaping our identity, discovery is not an adequate descriptor, and because we are not god-like, neither is construction. Instead, he argued that we fashion our identity, and are ourselves fashioned, through our relationships.[191] Exemplifying this, one interviewee talked about a time when his work colleagues had engaged him in conversations about his ordination journey, and how that had helped him to articulate his changing understanding of himself, in both the pre- and post-ordination phases. On the one hand, in reacting to their interest, he told stories (performance) to illustrate how his self-understanding and worldview were developing; on the other, he saw himself as engaged in a process of formation, through which he had developed his self-understanding as a PSW (discovery).

Although the precise mechanisms by which our identities form are complex, relationships are profoundly important in the process. Differentiating between collective forms of identity (such as gender, race, ethnicity and religion) and personal identity, Appiah emphasized the "dialogic nature of identity construction",[192] both through the relationship of the individual with significant others, and also with societal norms. As an African-American, Appiah (a British-Ghanaian philosopher who now regards himself as African-American) acknowledged the role of white American, as well as African-American, society and institutions in shaping African-American identity, arguing that finding—or not finding—our individual stories in the larger narratives available to us is part of whether we feel included or excluded. These larger societal narratives are "scripts" which "provide models for telling our lives".[193] Part of the power of such a script is that of naming, initiating processes of differentiation, and thereby providing identity, shaping what we feel is appropriate to that identity, and what is not.[194]

Difference can be a positive factor as we work out who we are, and where we fit in the communities of which we are part. If we accept that identity is formed in part at least through our interactions with others, then notions of a "pure" identity are untenable, since being in relationship with a number of different communities inevitably implies multiple identities (illustrated by Appiah's ironic recognition of the role of white culture in forming his African-American identity[195]). Difference and tension are therefore not necessarily undesirable. Towards the end of the final co-operative inquiry session, as we responded to the follow-up interview transcripts, we found ourselves discussing conflict and tension and transformation through the analogy of a violin string which has to be held in tension to make a sound. Tension arises between people or communities when there is difference, and yet both tension and difference are of value because they have the power to be transformative. Conflict is inevitable, but it does not have to be destructive, unless we allow it to be.

Who am I?

At an early stage in this research I encountered the work of Maggie Ross, the pen name of a Church of England solitary religious and theologian. Ross was critical of the clericalism which gives "those who wear collars or religious habits . . . privileged access to the higher wisdom of God", asserting that although church leaders "protest such assumptions, their unspoken signals often contradict their words".[196] She restricted use of cognates of the word "priest" to "the mirroring of God's kenotic, self-forgetful love, which is irreconcilable, in human terms, with self-reflective, functional power", using instead "presbyter" "for the middle position of threefold ordained ministry".[197] Priesthood is then not necessarily linked with ordination.[198]

Initially, I found myself in full agreement with what Ross was saying, particularly the argument that priesthood is not about function, but is about "self-effacement, self-forgetfulness, and humility",[199] and that all Christians are called to be priestly, to commit to a particular way of living. I cannot argue with her claim that "ordination *in itself* does not bestow the least spiritual authority, personal holiness, specialized knowledge of ways into God, or privileged access to God"[200]—indeed to do so would lack due humility. However, as I read on, I began to feel oppressed by her arguments, sensing that something very precious to me was being abused, although it took time for me to work out in detail why I was reacting in this way.

I have already described how an early sense of calling to ordained ministry ran aground in the 1970s, so it was a huge surprise to me when, around Easter 2005, I found myself in the cathedral talking to one of the residentiary canons, saying that I thought I had a call from God to ordained ministry. As my mouth opened and the words stumbled out, the rest of my mind was screaming "Stop! Shut up! Dig a deep hole, get in it, and bury yourself—right now!" But my mouth would not shut up, and in due course I found myself going through a lengthy and at times quite difficult and intrusive selection procedure. As I drove myself to the forty-eight-hour conference (Bishop's Advisory Panel) which would determine whether or not I would be recommended for training for ordination, I heard a song playing on my car CD player: "I'm going to meet my Lord". I felt excited, out of control and frankly terrified, as I wondered what on earth I was doing. I realized some time later that those were not the words of the song at all!

In August 2007, I commenced training, and I was ordained as a deacon in the Church of Christ in late June 2009. On the morning of my ordination as a deacon (a Saturday), I was awake very early, walking in a misty June dawn in the garden of the retreat house where we ordinands were staying. All through that day, I felt disoriented, dislocated even. On the Tuesday morning, after Sunday and Monday with my training incumbent in the parishes I was licensed to, I returned to my secular job—and felt disoriented all over again. During training I had experienced similar disorientation going from work on a Friday evening to residential weekends, then returning on Sunday afternoons to domesticity and work on Monday. It took time for the transitions to feel manageable, and to know how best to navigate them.

A year later, I was ordained priest. In the summer of 2005, knowing that I had set myself on a path which might end in ordination, I attended an ordination service in the cathedral for the first time. I was totally overwhelmed by what I heard and saw. One by one, the ordinands knelt in front of the bishop, who laid his hands on their heads. Immediately around them were a small group of other robed people placing a hand on the ordinands' shoulders and arms, and around them a host of other robed people all connecting to the ordinand as they put a hand on the shoulder, arm or back of the person in front of them. I could only imagine what it might feel like to be the person at the heart of this; I understood that something very powerful was happening.

When the time came for my own ordination as a priest, I slept well and there was no early-morning walk in the garden, for I knew much better what to expect this time. Kneeling in front of the bishop, as he laid hands on me, saying: "Send down the Holy Spirit on your servant, Jenny, for the office and work of a priest in your Church," I felt calm and at peace, at the centre of the prayers and support of a whole host of fellow priests. It was the following morning when I awoke early, nervous and excited, knowing that in a few hours I would celebrate the Eucharist for the first time. The church was absolutely full, with people from all of the five churches in the group that I served, as well as my family and friends. Part way through the Eucharistic Prayer, my colleague, who was acting as deacon, turned over two pages in my order of service at once. There was no part of my brain disengaged enough to notice, so I just continued for a short while, causing confusion to my husband, who was the organist for the service, and was waiting to play the music for the *Agnus Dei*.[201] It did not matter, we got back on track, and I realized that I was in the midst of something much greater than me or my mistakes.

Since that day, I have presided at the Eucharist many times. It is never routine, never a matter of going through the motions; always I am aware of leading the congregation in the presence of the living God, always I take a moment in the vestry to commit myself again to God as a priest in Christ's church. I am conscious as I robe and put on my stole that I am putting on God, inhabiting a holy place, sacred ground. Being ordained gave me the church's authority and the confidence to put myself in that place. This is not trivial, it goes to the very heart of my identity and my vocation: that is why Ross's dismissal of ordained priestly ministry was so offensive to me, and is one reason why I am doing this research.

Preparing in the vestry, standing behind the altar, priestly identity is clear; sitting at a desk, standing in front of a room full of students or teachers, what is it then?

Interviewees' perspectives on their identity as PSWs

Three remarks stood out in the interview data which prefaced interviewees' reflections on how they understand their identity as a PSW:

- I am ordained because . . .
- I call myself . . . because . . .
- I understand my vocation to be . . .

I am ordained because . . .
Graham Tomlin surmised in his account of giving a talk to a group of ordinands, who "included the whole spectrum, from evangelicals to charismatics to catholics", that it would be possible to have "a very strong idea of the identity of the priest", or equally to be "convinced of the priesthood of all believers".[202] Ordinands and priests with a strong sense of their priestly identity may well claim that ordination confers ontological change; they may come from a liberal catholic tradition or perhaps the Anglo-Catholic tradition. Others, for whom the priesthood of all believers is more important, may feel that their ordination is about function, rather than ontology, and may come from an evangelical or charismatic tradition.

I hesitate to generalize too much here, however. Despite my own years in the Baptist church, I would now describe myself as a liberal catholic, with quite a strong sense of the ontological transformation through the process of being ordained priest, and yet I still believe very strongly in the priesthood of all believers. The six interviewees came from different church and theological backgrounds. On the basis of what they said to me in our contextual discussions and in their interviews, I would say that three of the interviewees were from an evangelical background, and three were from a liberal catholic background. Differences in approach are apparent in the interview material, but, perhaps surprisingly, there is no correlation between church tradition and their understanding of their ordination.

I asked all of the interviewees why they had chosen to be ordained, in several instances prefacing my question with an account of a conversation in which I participated in my role as a diocesan officer for SSMs. I had been asked by a vocations adviser what my opinion was about recommending a potential candidate, given that this person intended to continue in their secular job after ordination, and that they could perfectly well continue any workplace ministry they might have without needing to be ordained. As Lees observed in his 2018 book on SSM: "Although the Church knows that many have a vocation, it's often hard for it see that a vocation might be centred on another sphere of work—and harder still to understand that ordination might enhance and complement it."[203]

An interviewee, who had been ordained in precisely this circumstance, said that:

> . . . the ultimate answer is, God decided that he [sic] wanted me to be ordained, and he appears to have decided that he wanted me to be ordained in the context in which I was then working, and largely still function. And, well, if that's what he wanted, then ultimately that's what he got.

She was not the only one to attribute the decision to go forward for ordination to a belief that this is what God wanted. Another told me that "I still feel that God was calling me for priesting from 1999", having earlier said that he saw his priesting as "a gift from God" which had happened just a few weeks before we met in the autumn of 2017. On the other hand, one interviewee said that his response to someone who asked why he needed to be a priest to do his work, was, "I don't have to be a priest, but I am, and what makes you ask about having to be?" The other five interviewees, whether from an evangelical or liberal catholic background, felt that their ordination involved ontological change:

> I'm ordained because that's what I felt called to be. It is ontological for me . . .

> When I was priested, I felt an extraordinary shock, as Bishop X laid his hands on me . . . And for me, that—yes, that's the symbol of that ontological change occurring.

> And I, from that day, really, thought I was a different person, and as I said, five years ago before I started, six years, before I started training, I'd have said, no, I wouldn't have seen that . . . I think, in that sense, it's right up there with that permanent change that is completely irreversible.

Church background made no difference to the kinds of things interviewees said about their ordination, and neither did length of time since ordination. One thing that did vary, however, was what they said about themselves and their role vis-à-vis Jesus. One interviewee said: "I think that we have the responsibility of acting in the way that Jesus would act, representing him here in physical form, in whatever we do." Another, however, commenting on WWJD wrist bands ("what would Jesus do?"), said: "There's some ontological differences between us and Jesus, actually," and that he wanted one which said: "Since when were you the Son of God?" In another interview, this exchange occurred:

> <So are you saying that the priest is standing in place of Christ as mediator?>
> I certainly wouldn't want to, that would seem to be unduly presumptuous. But I think that we do finally stand with Christ, and not in the place of Christ, in his and our facing of the world. Does that make sense?

In Chapter 4, I discussed the unease I felt at Christological interpretations of priesthood, and then described the sense of relief I experienced when I encountered a Trinitarian basis for priestly ministry, and so I particularly appreciated the way in which this interviewee expressed himself. However, what another interviewee said also resonates with my own feelings and experience:

> . . . when I could preside as a priest, and feel the Holy Spirit move through, that was the fulfilment of—and, as I say, so humbling that God had chosen me. . . . It's a gift from God to be in that place, to preside at the Eucharist, and to have the Holy Spirit go through . . .

The phrasing might be a little awkward, but his sense that this is not simply about him, but about the work of the Holy Spirit, is a reminder that in the end, there is no separating out Christ from the work of the Holy Spirit in and through us, and that God is not one, nor three, but is Trinity.

Moberly's argument (Chapter 4) rested in part on his Christological understanding of what happens in the Eucharist, but he also discussed at length what the effect of ordination is on a priest, claiming that the "'character' which is conferred, and is indelible, is a status, inherently involving capacities, duties, responsibility of ministerial life, yet separable from and, in a sense, external to the secret character of the personal self".[204] At least one of the interviewees appeared to agree with Moberly, that there is an indelible conferring of character at ordination, which is to be distinguished from the development of character which is inherent in going through a formative process, such as training for ordination:

> Because it's who I am, and it comes back to this ontological question: this is what I gave myself to be. In 1979 I said—or '80 I was priested—and I can't erase that from my character, if I can put it like that . . .

I understand this to say something about the effect on character of priestly formation, rather than the conferring of an external character, but I may be wrong. What other interviewees would have said about this, had I asked them, I cannot now determine, although some of them talked of being set aside in some way through ordination:

> I always felt a little apart . . .

> I mean, some people do need to be ordained, there is a setting apart even if you're in the middle of the mess, that somehow or other gets recognized.

> . . . one cannot escape that sense of call, set aside-ness . . .

This suggests quite a "high" view of priesthood, which Moberly would surely have recognized. He did not see priests as "intermediaries between the Body and its life. They do not confer life on the Body, in whole or in part", but he did believe that priests are "specifically representative for specific purposes and processes of the power of the life, which is the life of the whole body, not the life of some of its organs".[205] Given that he went on to say that the body needs all its organs and that the functionality of one organ cannot be given to a different organ, I interpret Moberly's argument to mean that while the origin of the life of the body of Christ depends on Christ, not on an ordained priesthood, nevertheless the priesthood has a necessary role in enabling that life. The source of the authority of the ordained priesthood is thus from God, and not from the church. This view was confirmed by one of the interviewees:

> I think what it [ordination] gave me was a confidence that I could speak with authority, and I don't mean the authority of a teacher, but that I had God, the Trinity, behind me and within me, when I was operating.

Others saw it as recognition by the church, or as something needed for the community:

> ... ordination is conferring something about the mind of the church ...

> I am a priest, but I'm a priest only really by virtue of being part of a college of clergy, because we are trying to be priests for the community ...

For all the interviewees, their ordination was highly significant, contributing to their sense of identity. Indeed for some, there was a sense that this was something they had needed in order to become fully themselves:

> I think when I was ordained a priest it was like, hah, now I am fully it.

> . . . being an ordained priest made a huge difference in all sorts of ways.

As we saw earlier, some would argue that identity is discovered, and hence already present in nascent form, others that it is constructed. Did the interviewees feel that their calling was initiated by God—suggesting that there is a priestly version of them that God wanted brought into being—or did they see it as their own choice under God—suggesting that it is an identity which they are free, under God, to construct? This was an issue which was discussed in the co-operative inquiry group, without our coming to any conclusions about it. Certainly, some of the interviewees understood their vocation to be initiated by God, and that their choice was whether to obey or not. Personally, I am aware that my ordination as a priest has fundamentally changed me from the person I was before, while being in continuation with my unordained self (as was the case with being married, having children, and becoming a teacher). In the end, I wonder if this is not similar to the discussion about being and doing, and that they are two sides of the same coin: in the doing is the becoming, and in choosing to do what I believe God is asking me to do, I become a person who chose to follow a path which resulted in ordination as a priest.[206]

I call myself . . . because . . .
What's in a name? The labels and names we are given, or which we apply to ourselves, contribute to forming our identity, and this contributed to the difficulty I had in deciding on an acronym.

According to the Church of England's website:

> Ministers in secular employment are deacons or priests whose ministry is focused in the workplace. Such ministers may be employed outside church life as nurses, engineers, teachers and in many other jobs.
>
> Ministers in secular employment tell the story of God's love in their workplaces, helping people make connections between life and faith through prayer, worship and reading the bible. They will

also preach, teach and enable God's people to be better disciples of Christ.[207]

This strikes me as inadequate in a number of ways, not least because the employment examples given are middle class vocational sorts of jobs, and there are many priests whose secular work is not obviously in this category. Furthermore, the description of the MSE gives no indication as to why such a person might want to be ordained, as it is equally applicable to the many lay people who are also ministers in secular employment, as the LLM who responded to my letter in the *Church Times* said (" . . . why it is thought that in situations where there is no sacramental ministry involved, a person can fulfil their calling as a Christian nurse, doctor, teacher, engineer, shopworker, whatever, better by being ordained priest?").

As can be seen from the quotations in the preceding section, the six interviewees in my research all saw their priestly ordination as a significant contributor to their identity. Talking about people who are ordained later in life, one interviewee observed:

> I guess it's in terms of your ontological understanding: am I first and foremost a priest, even though I might have been, in terms of time, a worker before that? And my secular job might continue without apparent interruption, but I have changed, and so I'm now first and foremost a priest.

This is also exemplified in this exchange from one of the follow-up interviews:

> <Is there anything that you think perhaps you should have emphasized more, or emphasized less [in the first interview]?>
> . . . the statement that really stood out . . . was—I am a priest. And I remember our conversation about what difference is it to be a Christian in the workplace, and to be a priest . . .
> <And thinking about it now, that statement "I am a priest", why does that stick out for you?>

Because in the workplace, you are—I was a teacher—and all the other responsibilities that I had, and labels[208]—and priest. And that, for me, couldn't be forgotten because it was who I am. I always felt a little set apart . . .

<You may or may not have noticed in the blurb I put in my online questionnaire, that I used the acronym M stroke PSE, because when I was first talking to people about this, I was just using minister in secular employment, as everybody else does. And then when I thought quite deeply about myself, I thought, it's really important to me that I'm a priest, not just a minister. And I just wonder whether you sort of saying "I am a priest" stuck out for you, or whether that's just me, or whether that's perhaps something that you might feel also?>

I didn't notice it during our conversation, but now you've raised it, I don't call myself a minister generally. I call myself a priest, which was a deliberate and conscious choice years ago, because my church is more—or it used to be—a lot more evangelical than probably it is now, and certainly than I am now. So the word "priest", it felt almost like a half-brave step to use it, but it has, for me, certain connotations that are important.

<Such as?>

Of being apart and called, and ordained for a purpose.

As I explained in this conversation, I had stopped using MSE, and started to use M/PSE, because of a discussion at an early stage of my research in which one person said that she felt more comfortable being called a minister, rather than a priest. M/PSE was therefore the term I used in the online questionnaire, and in all the documentation associated with the interviews. During the analysis of the interview transcripts, however, I became persuaded that although the interviewees generally used the accepted term, MSE, for themselves, what they were actually telling me was that they understood their priestly designation to be significant, and not one that could simply be subsumed under "minister".

Appiah has argued that there are cultural scripts which tell us how to be "male or female, black or white, gay or straight".[209] The interview excerpt above confirms my own feeling that the script that the Church of

England has for MSEs is deficient, not only because of the points made above, but also because it fails to acknowledge that there is a question to ask about the significance of priesthood for the MSE. If Appiah is correct, that adopting "an identity, [making] it mine is to see it as structuring my way through life",[210] then the question of what we are called is not trivial. A name or label, once given, has power, shaping both who we think we are, and also what others think appropriate for that sort of person.

The Church of England website sees the role of the MSE as one of "helping people make connections between life and faith through prayer, worship and reading the bible". This is not how the 1950s and 1960s worker priests interpreted their role, nor the 1970s NSMs. For the worker priests, it was about working alongside people who were unlikely to connect with the church in other ways, and was interpreted as a ministry of presence and accompaniment, rather than modelling discipleship as advocated by the Church of England. The 1970s NSMs found that trying to organize workplace Bible studies or prayer groups was not successful in the main,[211] and that much of their workplace ministry with non-churchgoers either took the form of pastoral support, or engagement in challenging discussions about topics such as the death of a child, or a devastating earthquake.[212]

As described in Chapter 4, there are three different models, other than that of the FTS, which emerged after the Second World War: the worker priest, who is a priest first but chooses menial, low-paid work as a form of incarnational ministry; the industrial chaplain, who may or may not be ordained, but is employed as a chaplain, not as a secular worker; and the NSM whose secular work preceded ordination, and who continues that work post-ordination. Despite this variety, in his 1983 report Hodge felt that the training for ministry at work provided by theological colleges was insufficient, and that "all the courses reported that they make no distinction in the training offered to those planning a non-stipendiary or a stipendiary ministry".[213] One of the complaints recorded in Hodge's report is that of a director of post-ordination training, who felt that because the people teaching the courses had little experience of secular work themselves, they would not know what they were talking about, and so it was inevitable that such training would be inadequate.[214] This is essentially still the case, for much the same reasons. It does not help that, in attempting to avoid complaints by SSMs that their ministry is not taken as seriously as that of FTSs, there is a tendency now to claim that all priests are the same, and so all need the same training.[215] This unhelpfully confuses equality of status with equality of provision of experience.

For four of my interviewees, ordination came later than establishing their secular careers, which continued without regard to their ordination. Although therefore not in the typical worker priest model, all four felt strongly that an incarnational ministry of presence was an important aspect of their self-understanding: as John Lees writes, "There is something incarnational and generous, too, in an understanding that God works *in* and *through* situations and people, not around them."[216] The other two interviewees do not fit any of the three models described above particularly well, as they were both ordained soon after university and initially served as full-time parish priests for a number of years, but over time came to believe that their vocation was to work in a professional secular capacity, while remaining priests licensed to a parish. Both of these talked about their lack of fit with acknowledged models.

One of the interviewees strongly identified with the worker priest model:

> <So would you see yourself in the line of the worker priests?>
>
> Yes. . . . they still exist, I mean, there are still younger ones coming through.
>
> . . . One or two of the original French ones are still alive, and until a few years ago more of them were still alive. . . . we still have close contact. The discussion is always the difference between the more European model, where they went into the lowest possible forms of employment, or even unemployment.
>
> < . . . it was a point of honour that they were not to be promoted into the managerial classes at all.>
>
> Yes. Most of us in the UK are actually middle class; we're—not all; there are some who aren't—but we are teachers and things of that sort. And I find the Europeans incredibly challenging, because they always force me to look back at who I am and what I'm doing.

She went on to describe how being a manager, and so considered "part of the enemy" by the European worker priests, gave her opportunities to make a difference in her workplace in ways which would not be accessible to the working class model of worker priest.

Are PSWs worker priests? Some of the PSWs I have spoken to, like the original French worker priests, are engaged in low-paid work which would not be described as a middle class type of employment, but they were not priests first, and their choice of employment tends to be more pragmatic—it is what is available to them—rather than a means of identifying with low-paid workers. Are PSWs like the 1960s British industrial chaplains? Not really, since they are employed to do a job, and are not generally employed to be chaplains, although a few are paid to offer chaplaincy services in addition to their other duties. Are PSWs like the NSMs of the 1970s? This model is much closer to where most PSWs today are located in that their secular work predates their ordination and continues post-ordination, and some of the issues identified by the 1970s NSMs were mentioned by people in my research. However, few of the 1970s NSMs chose to hold together both secular work and ministry in tension in the long term, whereas many of today's PSWs keep both going, either out of choice, or because there is no easy way to resolve the tension. We are not chaplains, paid to minister; we are not indistinguishable from FTSs, other than in not being paid; we are not worker priests, committing ourselves to a ministry of presence with low-paid workers; and we are not MSEs of the model described on the Church of England website, providing a churchy model of discipleship in our workplaces. None of these models is a perfect fit, and so none of the names/labels is a good fit either.

I understand my vocation to be ...
The interviewees understood God's call on their lives as a call to be ordained as priests, while continuing to work in their secular occupations. One described nervously going to a meeting with the bishop who she hoped would sponsor her as an ordinand:

... by that stage I already felt called to carry on working in school, and for that to be the main focus of my ministry, unofficially, I wasn't going as a school chaplain or anything ...

And it all fell into place as if God were at work, because Bishop X obviously didn't have a problem with me being ordained at all; and in fact, said he'd given my situation consideration, and he felt that I ought to carry on working in teaching full-time and that ought to be the focus of my ministry. And that I had things to bring to state education, particularly in a town like ...

The detail of each interviewee's vocation is specific to them, but they all shared a sense that they were called by God to be that person, and that that they have one vocation, not several:

Starting from the point that you are a priest all the time, you are not simply a priest in certain places or in particular contexts, you're a priest all the time. That does quite a lot in terms of integration, but the other side of it comes from the people who ask you, "Well, how do you manage to be a priest and do all that?", to which the answer is, "It's not *and*, it's not be a priest *and* do all that. It's—I do all this *because* I am a priest. I do all this and I am a priest, they're all just inextricably linked together." It's not just turning up to church on Sunday and putting some funny robes on, and saying some rather weird and ancient words. And I don't—a lot of the time, I don't do what you might look at, I mean, I don't, have never, run prayer groups at work, or done anything like that. It's about the whole of your life is your service to God; the whole of your life is your vocation, whatever you happen to be doing. [original verbal emphases]

Because I'm one person and I am a priest, what I'm doing, it's as a priest. Even if it's not obviously priestly and I'm not wearing robes or a collar, I am a priest in whatever I do, and I'm mindful of that wherever I am.

As these excerpts indicate, there is no split in identity. Every PSW I have spoken to, or interviewed, has affirmed that their priesthood is the lens through which everything else they do should be understood, regardless of the context or location or nature of what they are doing. Wherever they are, whatever they are doing, it is as a priest.

Conclusion: Priestly identity

The focus of this chapter is the question the priests and Levites, sent out from Jerusalem to see what was going on in the wilderness, put to John the Baptist: "Who are you?" In reflecting on that question for myself, I recognize four key influences which have brought me to where I am now: my family, being a teacher, being ordained priest, and God; and it was essentially the same for the six interviewees, with the appropriate professional identity substituted.

One way in which we construct our identities is through difference.[217] It was quite common for interviewees to clarify what they felt they were not, as a way of saying something about who they were. One interviewee emphasized that she has never been the sort of SSM whose secular work is only important in so far as it supports them financially: her work mattered to her for itself, and her ministry is a gift for which she has never been, nor wished to be, paid. This was also important to another interviewee, who likened himself to St Paul, working to provide for himself. Another used the example of an FTS that he knew, as a way to emphasize that far from being a part-time priest, his commitment was greater, because the FTS would refuse to take funerals on his day off, whereas for the PSW time away from his secular work was time for parish-based ministry.

Our calling, the PSW vocation, is not in the end about the church, but about all of life: it is about participating in the *missio Dei*: we are committed to the institutional church and to our secular work and workplaces. One interviewee summed it up as "the sacrament of offering up daily life for myself and others in the Eucharist—not always at an altar—but in, so to speak, Eucharistic moments when the everyday, the quotidian, becomes sacred". That sacramental aspect (explored in greater depth in Chapter 10) is why this book is about *priests* in secular work.

While I know that in some dioceses, there are "permanent" deacons—people who are ordained deacon, but who do not expect to be ordained priest—who are considered to have a ministry which bridges the church and the secular world, my feeling is that this is a different vocation from the priest in secular work, and that neither is to be subsumed into the other. The people I interviewed were all very clear that they were priests as well as deacons because of that sacramental focus.

We are priests whose secular work is part of our vocation, who seek to serve God in all aspects of our lives, and that is the focus of the next chapter.

CHAPTER 9

What do you seek?

> The next day John [the Baptist] again was standing with two of his disciples, and as he watched Jesus walk by, he exclaimed, "Look, here is the Lamb of God!" The two disciples heard him say this, and they followed Jesus. When Jesus turned and saw them following, he said to them, "What are you looking for?" ... One of the two who heard John speak and followed him was Andrew, Simon Peter's brother. He first found his brother Simon and said to him, "We have found the Messiah" (which is translated Anointed).
>
> John 1:35-38a,40-41

In the Gospel tradition, an important aspect of John the Baptist's role is to point to Jesus (John 1:20; cf. Matthew 3:11). According to John the Evangelist, on hearing what John the Baptist said about Jesus, two of his disciples, one of whom was Andrew, were sufficiently convinced to follow Jesus. Realizing they were there, Jesus asked them what they were looking for, or as the King James Bible renders it: "What seek ye?" Andrew recognized that they had found the Messiah, and immediately went to find his brother, Simon: for it was the Messiah that they were seeking.

In the first paragraph of his *Confessions*, Augustine wrote: "*cor nostrum inquietum est donec requiescat in Te*", which my English translation renders as "our hearts find no peace until they rest in you".[218] In *Befriending our Desires*, Philip Sheldrake claimed that "desire lies at the heart of what it is to be human".[219] The quotation from Augustine is one that has resonated for me ever since I first read it many years ago, and reading Sheldrake's work confirmed my sense that there is something important here: that the desire for the ultimate (God), and the restlessness we experience in the absence of knowing God, underlie so much of our motivation for what we do and what we seek. In my conversations with PSWs, I was left in no doubt that the ground of all the being, doing and seeking that we discussed was our sense that it is about God, and our seeking of God through our calling to be PSWs: like Andrew and his companion, we too seek the Messiah.

Sheldrake wrote: "There is an energy within all of us that haunts us and can either lead us to set out on a quest for something more or can frustrate us by making us nostalgic for what we do not have."[220] In the next section, I explore my own sense of seeking, situating my choice of the question "what do you seek?" in my own experience, which provides a basis for the interpretation of the PSW that follows in the rest of this chapter.

What do I seek?

My maternal grandparents, born in 1898 and 1899 respectively, married in their early twenties and moved away from their families in rural Norfolk, not, as far as I remember from my mother's stories, to be with anyone they already knew or to take up some specific form of employment, but simply to better themselves. Settling into what was then a rural Buckinghamshire village, they raised their family of five children, including my mother, who was born there. My father's family arrived there a few years later, when he was ten, and so I grew up in a small community where everyone knew my grandparents, my parents, and our wider family, and everyone knew me.

I left the village of my childhood twice. My first leaving was at the age of eighteen for university. Although to start with I returned during the vacations, I married a fellow undergraduate at the end of our second year, and we set up home (in successively more squalid, but cheaper, flats) in our university city. After graduation, we initially stayed put, moving on two years later so that I could attend a Baptist theological college. During that time, at a reunion with friends from undergraduate days, one commented how much she thought I had changed, that I was much more restful to be around. I did indeed experience a sense of "finding myself" when I started at the Baptist college, but, sadly, as has already been described, that did not last.

I returned to the village, where my parents and maternal grandfather still lived, about nine years after leaving the first time, with two small children and a husband who frequently worked away from home. I wanted something of that security I had known as a child for my own children, the security of being known and rooted—not to mention having a devoted granny on hand! However, perhaps it was more the devoted granny than anything else that kept me there for the next six years, during which I had two more children. Village life began to feel claustrophobic—my parents were pillars of the local Baptist church and the Memorial Hall, and we would follow in their footsteps, of course. Perhaps the weight of expectations contributed to my enthusiasm, when opportunity offered, to accompany my husband to the USA, initially for a period of three months, and ultimately for almost six months.

We would have stayed longer, perhaps permanently even, but for my mother, who found the absence of her grandchildren unbearable. Instead, some two years after our return to the UK, we moved to an isolated farmhouse in the Peak District—beautiful in summer, a nightmare in winter. When we first saw our farmhouse, it was spring; on the evening of the summer's day we moved in, I looked away towards the horizon and saw layer after layer of dark peaks, merging into the darkening sky. I was beguiled by the sense of being on the edge, reaching out restlessly to what I did not know. But we had no roots there; we were not known; we were incomers to be idly talked about, then forgotten. Away from everyone who really knew us, our lives fell apart. Winter brought snow and isolation, and an increasingly fragile marriage could not take the strain.

Needing to find a way forward for myself and my children, I decided the answer was teaching, so applied to do a course of study leading to the Post-Graduate Certificate in Education. As an initial assignment, I was asked to write an account of what had brought me to that point. That account no longer exists (there were no personal computers in those days, with everything saved on an external hard drive), but I remember ending it, saying something like: "So that is how I come to be where I am now, hoping that finally I have found my way forward." My tutor commented that she had very much enjoyed reading my account, hoping that I had enjoyed writing it (I had), but that she did not believe in final endings. Thinking about that comment now, I wonder if I was actually trying to articulate my need to satisfy the restlessness inside me.

After the farmhouse, my children and I moved frequently until I remarried (my eldest daughter once told me how many primary schools she went to—guilt prevents me from recalculating it). With my second marriage came stability, and my children grew up and moved away to university in their turn. Our final move came about when I left classroom teaching to work in a university department some fifty miles away, and we moved to Ely where we now live: we will have been here for two decades before too long, and we have no intention of going anywhere else.

The sense of being unrooted, of seeking . . . something, was satisfied to a large extent by the experience of a good marriage and satisfying work, although I was aware that part of the attraction for me in being a school teacher was that no two days were ever alike. My sense of restlessness did not disappear entirely, but was channelled into recognizing that my teaching was never perfect, that there would always be a better way to teach a topic (I never understood how anyone could use last year's teaching notes, always starting from scratch when planning my lessons).

When I left classroom teaching to work in a schools' enrichment project, I was freed from the pressure of trying to get students through high stakes examinations. Preparing resources for other teachers to use gave me the opportunity to present different ways into mathematical concepts, often through exploring connections with other curriculum areas. I felt fulfilled by my work, realizing that I was no longer looking around for something else. I could attribute this to age, but I am sure that the sense that I was using my God-given gifts to create the means by which others could find patterns and connections, and express them through maths, was more important. I felt that I was like the servant in the parable who was given five talents and doubled them (Matthew 25:14–30; Luke 19:12–27), that I was working with the grain of the universe. Following my ordination, I gradually became aware that this was not separate from my sense of vocation to priestly ministry, but was an important way in which that vocation would be expressed. My secular work, both in education and in research, mattered hugely to me, and, I believe, to God, and so my vocation was to be a PSW.

I cannot express it any better than these words from Charles Wesley's hymn, "O Thou Who Camest From Above":

> Jesus, confirm my heart's desire
> To work and speak and think for Thee;
> Still let me guard the holy fire,
> And still stir up Thy gift in me.

I chose this hymn for the service in which I first celebrated the Eucharist, and we have sung it at each of my licensing services since. It is a prayer which, I believe, finds its answer in my being a PSW, including through the research on which this book is based.

Theology of work

My secular work was important to me, both as means of expressing who I am, and as a means of putting some of my gifts at the service of others. As I talked to other PSWs, those in the co-operative inquiry group, my interviewees, and many others since, I have found that same recognition in them, that our secular work is a key way in which we live out our priestly vocations. Dorothy L. Sayers argued that the natural function of humans made in the image of God is to work, and it should therefore be considered primary.[221] Similarly, Alain de Botton celebrated work as "a hymn to the intelligence, peculiarity, beauty and horror of the modern workplace and, not least, its extraordinary claim to be able to provide us, alongside love, with the principal source of life's meaning".[222]

If such claims have any substance, then work should be a major focus for theology. The centrality of work to human life has not, however, been reflected in the numbers of studies of the theology of work until recently, although following Vatican II and *Laborem exercens* (1981) it did gain importance.[223] Work is always to an extent functional, and it is also necessarily formative for the person doing it, but what *Laborem exercens* claimed was that work is far more than this, because it involves human co-creation with God. Key issues for a theology of work to consider, therefore, are the purpose of work and how it might contribute to the transformation of this age through the *missio Dei*. Is it reasonable to claim that our work matters because it is a gift from God, and it is the means by which we are transformed as we work with God in transforming God's creation,[224] or is this over-stating the case?

Work in the Bible

The Bible is ambivalent about work: on the one hand deeming it given by God and so good (Genesis 2:15), but on the other, as sweat and toil (Genesis 3:19).[225] In the Ancient Near East, labour was not seen as worthy of the divine, and the account of creation in the first chapters of Genesis is quite atypical.[226] God's work in creation establishes the value of work, and the value of rest, and so it is reasonable to see this as the rhythm for the human beings made in God's image (Genesis 1:26–7), given that the "Lord God took the man and put him in the garden of Eden to till it and keep it" (Genesis 2:15). With his expulsion from Eden, however, Adam's work is reduced to toil, as is reinforced in the story of Cain, when God refuses to accept his offering, and work becomes drudgery (Genesis 4:3–5,12). With the migration to Egypt, and the subsequent enslavement of the Israelites, work is not simply toil and drudgery, but hard labour, with no possibility of sabbath rest (Exodus 5). The restoration of the people in the wilderness also restores work as a blessing (e.g. Exodus 31:1–11), as the people are given detailed instructions by God to make the ark of the covenant (Exodus 25) and the tabernacle (Exodus 26), both signifying God's presence with the people.

In the wilderness, ordinances were given to Moses, and a core theme of Leviticus is that because God is holy, so the people of Israel were to be holy (Leviticus 11:45), shaped by their obedience to those ordinances. In Leviticus, we can see what God wants for God's people in their working lives: access to meaningful work in which humans cooperate with God, ensuring that everyone has enough (e.g. Leviticus 19:9–10), and where there is provision for distorted relationships to be restored (e.g. Leviticus 6:4–5; 19:18). Indeed, it has been claimed that Leviticus is a necessary background to Jesus' teaching about work for that very reason.[227]

While we know that Jesus said he needed to do the work for which his Father had sent him (e.g. John 9:4), and that this occupied the three years of his public ministry, it is easy to miss the fact that he must have spent many years prior to that working as a carpenter (Mark 6:3). Jesus used examples from everyday work in his parables, such as a farmer who sowed seed (Matthew 13:1–23), a woman sweeping as she searched for a lost coin (Luke 15:8–10), a shepherd who looked for a lost sheep (Luke 15:3–7), builders who built on sand and on rock (Luke 6:46–49), vineyard workers (Matthew 20:1–16), and many others. However, while Jesus took it for granted that his hearers would recognize such working contexts, in the Sermon on the Mount he warned against putting undue priority on daily concerns, such as what to eat and drink, and what to wear, illustrating his point with the lilies of the field which "neither toil nor spin" (Matthew 6:25–33).

Work is largely incidental in the rest of the New Testament, although according to John Taylor it is a key theme in 1 Thessalonians:[228]

> You remember our labour and toil, brothers and sisters; we worked night and day, so that we might not burden any of you while we proclaimed to you the gospel of God.
> *1 Thessalonians 2:9*

We know from Paul's own writings, and from Acts, that at times he supported himself by working with his hands (e.g. Acts 18:1–3; 20:33–35; Philippians 4:14–16), urging others to do the same (1 Thessalonians 4:11). In 2 Thessalonians 3:6–15, the readers are exhorted to follow Paul's example in not being a burden on anyone, but rather to work to support themselves (the authorship of 2 Thessalonians is disputed,[229] but this does not detract from the point made). Paul both worked himself, and expected others to do the same, so that in contributing to ministry and evangelism, he and his companions were not burdens on anyone else.

Work in the Christian tradition

Work was perceived as important in the monastic tradition, although the rationale behind that varied. Benedict's Rule for monks living communally dates from the sixth century, and recommends a regular rhythm of prayer, sacred reading, manual work and rest.[230] Manual work was included to ensure that the monks were not idle ("the enemy of the soul"), and so that they could "live by the labour of their hands, as did our Father and the Apostles".[231] Thomas Aquinas gave four reasons for human work: to obtain food, to avoid the idleness which is a cause of sin, to restrain oneself from lust and desire, and for almsgiving.[232] Like Benedict, he favoured a regular regimen of work and prayer in monastic life, where the work could be manual labour, administration, teaching or writing. Work was what a person did to obtain the necessities which would allow him [sic] to contemplate God, and a means of subduing the passions which might keep him from God, and so was a means to an end, not an end in itself. The contemplative life, on the other hand, "is simply more excellent than the active . . . [because] the active life is occupied with externals" and "the contemplative life is more delightful than the active".[233]

A key factor in the Protestant Reformation was *sola fide*, Luther's assertion that justification before God is by faith alone, and that we cannot work our way into the kingdom of God. Reacting against the monastic culture which he had rejected, he deemed all vocations to be equal, with the cloister no better than anywhere else, because all are called to share Christ's earthly ministry, serving others out of love, whether by milking cows, cutting hay, or cooking meals.[234] In this way, Luther linked the daily work of every Christian with their divine calling.[235]

At the time of writing, a search on the Church of England website for "work" led to links featuring the work of the Church of England or General Synod, or working with children and young people or with others nationally or internationally. Using the key phrase "secular employment" provided a link to "No ordinary ministry", advice on supporting candidates for ordination through selection, and (bizarrely) a page about trees in your churchyard. "No ordinary ministry" features links to further information about a range of different forms of ministry, including, below "Missionary work" and just above "Churchwardens and parish officers", "Ministers in secular employment", with the subtitle "Taking the gospel into the workplace".[236]

Neither work as a means to the leisure to contemplate God (Aquinas), nor work as vocation (Luther), considers the effect of human work on the creation and on us, and neither does the Church of England's website, with its focus on the church's ministry. One contemporary source I have been able to find that acknowledges issues such as the contribution of work to the *missio Dei*, or the effect of work on the individual and on society, is the London Institute of Contemporary Christianity. On their website, "work" is one of the main links, taking the reader straight through to a page entitled "Your Work Matters to God", which hosts a number of different links and articles.[237]

Work as an eschatological category
Over seventy years ago, the writer Dorothy L. Sayers asserted that work should be "a way of life in which the nature of man [sic] should find its proper exercise and delight and so fulfil itself to the glory of God".[238] She went on to affirm that work should be seen as "a creative activity undertaken for the love of the work itself; and that man, made in God's image, should make things, as God makes them, for the sake of doing well a thing that is well worth doing". However, in both Catholic and Protestant theology, prior to the final decades of the twentieth century, work, despite its importance in all our lives, was considered to be a secondary category, a means to an end. Change was signalled when, in *Laborem exercens*, John Paul II claimed that "human work is *a key,* probably *the essential key,* to the whole social question, if we try to see that question really from the point of view of man's [sic] good . . . the key, namely human work, [thus] acquires fundamental and decisive importance".[239]

The first significant reference in the twentieth century for a theology of work is Karl Barth's *Church Dogmatics* III/4, published in 1951, which concerns the doctrine of creation.[240] Barth placed work within the doctrine of creation under the heading of sabbath, so that sabbath is a pre-condition for work, not simply about rest after work. He would not have subscribed to more recent claims that human work can be considered as co-creation with God, however, asserting that human work was not to be understood as an extension of God's creation, since God's work is always complete.[241] The first person to present anything like a comprehensive theology of work was the worker priest, Marie-Dominique Chenu,[242] who claimed, without citing his evidence, that the term came into use "five or six years ago".[243] He rejected the use of outmoded images for workers, such as the potter, the blacksmith and the peasant, on the grounds that these were not only inadequate, but that they "often encouraged a resentment against the machine and led to debatable praise of craft-working, small-scale proprietorship, the patriarchal family and the peasantry, which is both bad theology and vain romanticism".[244] He asserted that work is not simply about earning a living, but is also a means by which we serve one another.[245] However, although he saw work as of value in itself, it "is not, of course, an end in itself in which man [sic] finds his final achievement, as in a Marxist dictatorship of the proletariat".[246] For Chenu, work was neither "a means of perfection, nor a mere collection of utilities, advantages and prosperities which pious intentions will endow with morality", but "is a purpose in its rightful place, a secondary purpose".[247]

Chenu experienced at first hand what it was like to work in dehumanizing conditions, where the worker was simply another cog in the machine. He considered such work to be "degrading" and against God's purposes, because the focus was on the product at the expense of the worker.[248] It is ironic, therefore, that Chenu was among the French worker priests suppressed in 1953 because they were deemed to be communists. Despite this, in the 1960s he was one of the theologians whose work informed Vatican II, and his views on work are echoed by John Paul II in *Laborem exercens*.[249] Chenu's theology of work opened the way to creation being seen as continuous, rather than completed, and of human work understood as co-creation with God.[250]

Laborem exercens built on Chenu's argument, while managing to avoid what has been called his rather "uncritical celebration of technology, modernity and progress".[251] On the other hand, one could claim that *Laborem exercens* romanticized toil by claiming it as participation in Christ's suffering.[252] Nevertheless, the concept of co-creation, originating in Chenu's writing, and an important aspect of *Laborem exercens*, has featured in much subsequent theological discussion of work. Not all recent theologians agree with such views, however. Hauerwas, for one, has been highly critical, seeing *Laborem exercens* as "a disaster both in the general perspective it takes toward work as well as its specific arguments".[253] Like Barth, Stanley Hauerwas argued that God completed his work prior to the Fall and so human work is of a different order, and that "the theological analysis of work is deficient, and this results in a social and economic theory that systematically distorts the nature and significance of work in most people's lives". He further deemed John Paul II's understanding of work to be "theologically arbitrary, romantic, elitist, and certainly an insufficient basis for an adequate social theory or critique". Hauerwas also critiqued what he saw as the exclusive use of Genesis 1–3 in *Laborem exercens* for its scriptural basis, which is somewhat unfair, as there are other biblical references.

In *Work in the Spirit*, Volf wanted to do for a Protestant theology of work what *Laborem exercens* had done for a Catholic theology of work.[254] Alert to the need to avoid romanticizing work, he claimed that "theology of work is a critical theological reflection onto the reality of human work",[255] where that reality includes child labour, unemployment, discrimination, dehumanization, exploitation, and the effects of all these on the environment.[256] This reality is multi-layered, affecting both individuals and society more generally; it is both structural and technological.[257] Volf considered that an inductive approach, starting from the Bible, was problematic because work is never considered as a primary theme—there is a difference between biblical teaching about work and a theology of work—and the context of work in the modern age is so very different from that of past ages.[258] Having been a student of Jürgen Moltmann's, Volf followed his eschatological focus in locating the theology of work in the new creation, seeing the task as not simply interpreting work from a Christian perspective, but showing how it can be transformed by the Spirit for the new creation.[259]

For both Volf and *Laborem exercens*, the fundamental question is whether there is continuity between this present age and the age to come. If there is a radical discontinuity, then nothing now is of ultimate significance, including work, other than in how it fits us for participation in the new creation. If, on the other hand, there is continuity of some kind, implying eschatological transformation rather than annihilation, then work does have ultimate significance.[260] There are echoes here of Irenaeus' refutation of gnostic heresies of the first and second centuries: "Neither is the substance nor the essence of the creation annihilated (for faithful and true is He who has established it)."[261] If we take it as given, that whatever is worthwhile of this age will be transformed rather than annihilated in the age to come, then our work matters.

Theologically, work can be grounded either in the first things or in the last things—protologically or eschatologically.[262] Volf preferred the eschatological basis on the grounds that Christianity is essentially eschatological because the new creation is the *telos* of the first creation, and because human work does not simply maintain what God creates, but transforms it through the work of the Holy Spirit.[263] The vocation of the Christian, therefore, should not to be reduced to church-based activity, but should involve using the gifts of the Spirit in daily work.[264] The work of non-Christians also has the potential to be transformed, since all human work, whoever performs it, will pass through the purifying judgement of God in order that it can contribute to the new creation.[265]

In the biblical texts, as discussed above, work was always part of the divine plan for human beings made in God's image, but, as a consequence of the Fall, is distorted into toil and drudgery. A reductive focus on work as toil and drudgery, however, ignores its potential to be so much more, if we understand our work as an end in itself, not simply the means to some other end.[266] As *Laborem exercens* asserted, at its best, work "is not only good in the sense that it is useful or something to enjoy; it is also good as being something worthy".[267] Centuries earlier, Irenaeus argued that as created beings, humans have to grow into the full likeness of God,[268] and through their "work . . . realize and grow into who they were created to be".[269] Christ shows us how to do that.[270]

Materialist and utilitarian understandings of human work have tended to focus on nature as a resource for humans, rather than part of God's creation and so sufficient in itself, and on work as no more than the means by which humans survive.[271] *Laborem exercens* was not entirely free from such: the argument that work is good for human beings because "through work man *[sic] not only transforms nature*, adapting it to his own needs, but he also *achieves fulfilment* as a human being and indeed, in a sense, becomes 'more a human being'"[272] would be better expressed in a way that is more respectful of the non-human creation.

Utilitarian views are at the heart of many issues about work. Where an organization prioritizes its product and efficiency and profit at the expense of its workers' welfare, then that organization has set up gods to worship.[273] There is nothing new in this (cf. the Egyptian enslavement of the Israelites), but "it is still plausible to claim that never before has it enjoyed such a triumphant extension to become almost effectively the total worldview of an entire culture as in the modern West" where human worth is "measured in terms of profit and efficiency . . . [and] [a]bsolute utility reveals itself as nothing but violent self-interest and nihilism".[274] It is not hard to join the dots that connect an undue focus on profit to the exploitation, and even enslavement, of human beings.

A theology of work should also address the perfection which is the enemy of the good, and the expectation that all work will point beyond itself to God, neither of which is achievable prior to the *eschaton*, and the necessity for structures and institutions to be redeemed as well as individuals.[275] Another issue is the *de facto* inference that the kingdom of God is within the church, with the world outside the church beyond God's remit; the corollary, that holiness is a church-based virtue, is equally unhelpful. Alongside this is the assumption that church-based work is better than secular work for the Christian disciple, thus devaluing much of what any of us, lay or ordained, may contribute to God's kingdom through our secular work.

Interviewees' perspectives on finding God in and through their work

Here is a brief summary. The PSW seeks God by looking for evidence of God at work in the world (the *missio Dei*), and especially in and through their secular work. The PSW wants to work with God in and through work which is perceived to be God-given, using their God-given gifts, which is the way in which they can participate in the *missio Dei*. Because the PSW seeks God in their everyday work, they understand that not only is it necessary to "get their hands dirty", but that it is part of the PSW's vocation to enable others to see God at work in the "dirtiness" of everyday, secular life. The PSW also understands that this requires them to accept that there may be a personal cost to this seeking of God.

Seeking God in the world

"There's a whole way of looking at life if you factor in even covertly the God of Jesus Christ": so said one of the interviewees. The context was his assertion that the "acid test for anything we do here" is "how does this proclaim Christ to the world?" This particular question was specifically addressed in one of the four PSW narratives in Chapter 7, but here I want to focus on that way of looking at life which is about seeking God through factoring in the God of Jesus Christ. In the Gospel account, we read how Andrew, having encountered Jesus, went running to find his brother, Simon, to tell him that he and his companion had found the Messiah, that they had found that for which they were seeking. For us, who live "in the theological interim between Pentecost and the Parousia", the task is to "work out where God is", to find the Messiah in our context. While acknowledging the challenges of this, the interviewees felt that it was a key part of their vocation to be people who had to engage with this task, and, through this, to enable others to do the same; it is about helping lay Christians "to see and feel that everything that they do is part of vocation", so that "people in their working lives feel that they are building the kingdom, one way or another".

In 2011, a university employee, Diana Garfield, submitted her PhD thesis on how lay Christians acknowledged, or not, their faith in their workplace.[276] She claimed that for many lay Christians, the difficulty in making connections between everyday working life and what happens in church on Sundays leads people to compartmentalize them. The Church of England has over recent years realized that there is indeed work to be done in helping people to take their faith outside of the "Sunday box" into the "weekday box". *Setting God's People Free* was an initiative by the Archbishops' Council designed "to enable the whole people of God to live out the Good News of Jesus confidently in all of life, Sunday to Saturday".[277] This initiative seeks to help people look beyond the institutional church for the context in which they live out their faith, so not limiting "vocation to church-based roles". More recently, a section entitled *Everyday Faith* has been added to this. Sadly, I cannot find any mention anywhere in these webpages of an existing resource in the Church of England, namely a group of people who have already had to do considerable hard thinking in precisely this area.

The question about what it means to look for God and proclaim God in the secular is one which it is easy to answer in a superficial way, so losing sight of deeper issues. Although the word "proclaim", used by one interviewee, might suggest overt evangelization, it was more nuanced than that for all the interviewees.[278] All of them were open about their ordination as priests, in that their secular colleagues all knew, but for some that was as far as it could go, since any indication that they were engaged in evangelizing others in the workplace would have precipitated disciplinary proceedings. One, a counsellor, talked about how he would make "God explicit within the situation, without necessarily the other person in the situation having any grasp of what I was thinking or pointing to". When I asked him to explain what he meant by this—since I could not see how God could be made explicit in such a way—he continued:

> I think explicit can be explicit to self, but also I could make God explicit by making the love of God, which is implicit anyway, explicit or more explicit to that person, without it being obvious to that person that we're actually talking about the divine *per se*.

I interpret this argument to mean equating the presence of God and the love of God, both expressed in and through the care and respect the interviewee would give to his clients. God's name does not need to be explicitly mentioned for God to be present and active through love, which is God's self-expression. This interpretation is confirmed by something the interviewee said later: "God expresses himself [sic] . . . not only through those who are aware of him, but also through those who are not aware of him." This view was also articulated by another interviewee, talking of a colleague who is a self-confessed atheist, but whom the interviewee saw as part of the work of God in their workplace, through their mutual involvement in support of colleagues.

The interviewee did not claim that making God explicit (however done) was the exclusive preserve of the PSW; indeed, he was careful not to do so, because "if you are a priest, or even maybe a Christian in the workplace and taking your faith seriously, you are plunged into that, it is asked of you". However, he felt that for FTSs (having been one himself):

> ... there is so much in stipendiary ministry that is both busy and really rather ecclesiastical. And so the notion for a stipendiary priest that one might spend a significant part of your time seeing God as he *[sic]* is made manifest by himself in the world, in a way that is not actually terribly obvious—it's rather difficult to do that from a stipendiary point of view, I think.

Early in his interview, I had asked him to tell me about "the difference between being an MSE, and between being a parish priest". He responded:

> ... the thing I loved about MSE was having to make sense of it as a Christian vocation, as a seeking of God in God's world, as a seeking of the resurrection of Christ in God's world, in settings that were non-religious, by and large.

Later in our conversation, he expressed it thus:

> ... the non-stipendiary ministry is important, but MSE is not merely non-stipendiary, it's secular. I think if—oh, well, that's it, at a profound but simple level, it asserts that religion is secular as well as religious. Otherwise, one comes across people, clergy and laity alike, who trap ... into quotes the religious.
> <Put it into the Sunday box, you mean?>
> Or into very religious categories that are—that go unchallenged.

In Chapter 2, discussing what we mean by the categories "sacred" and "secular", I quoted words written by Etty Hillesum,[279] in which she affirmed the potential for everything to be sacred, together with an article in the *Church Times*, in which Eve Poole wrote that there is no secularity because "God made the world, and Christ redeemed it".[280] This argument depends on what precisely is meant by "secular":[281] is it that which is beyond redemption, or is it that which is beyond the bounds of the institutional church? For the PSW, it is important, with Hillesum, to recognize the potential for finding the sacred in the most unlikely places, and with Poole, to believe that nowhere is beyond Christ's redemption.

Indeed, being a PSW "is not merely what some people do with their ministry, or one of many patterns of ministry . . . it actually reflects a whole theological pattern for thinking about God, that he's *[sic]* relevant also to, well, the whole of creation", as one interviewee put it. I feel this is a really important point to make, that the PSW is "not merely non-stipendiary", but "secular". The secular is not beyond God's redemption, and one way in which God's presence in the secular is made apparent is through the presence there, and the work, of the PSW.

Seeking God through work

If the PSW is called to seek God in the world outside the church, then that clearly includes the workplace. However, I want to go beyond affirming the PSW's vocation to seek God in people or in places, and to consider their vocation to seek God through their secular work.

One of the co-operative inquiry group was ordained priest in her early twenties, but later decided to exercise her priestly vocation part-time in the church, and part-time through her own business; the other three (myself included) had been ordained towards the end of successful secular careers. Similarly, for four of the interviewees, ordination did not present them with an alternative to their pre-existing secular work, but would be something they needed to understand as part of a vocation which included that secular work. The other two interviewees had started out as FTSs, leaving parish ministry to become PSWs because they came to see their priestly vocation as including secular work. One of these was still in full-time secular work at the time of our interview; the other had decided to return to full-time parish ministry for the final five years of his working life after many years in secular work.

It became clear early in the inquiry group discussions that our secular work mattered to us all, so during the morning I spent with each interviewee, I asked them specifically about their secular work: what they did, for how long they had been doing it, and why they had not given it up for full-time parish ministry. Answering, one of the teachers told me an anecdote about an occasion when she was having lunch with her husband in a pub, which she later repeated in the recorded interview:

> ... this man came up to me and he said, "I'm in the Merchant Navy now, because of you.... You were so strict, and you made me work and I got that B, and without it I'd have never been able to do what I always wanted." And that kind of thing happens to me, not a lot, not every time I go out, but enough times for me to feel, well, I did it right.

She believed that her work as a teacher mattered, because:

> ...a good education allowed a person to become the person God ordained them to be. I mean, ordained in its widest sense—God designed them to be, made them to be.... And I drove myself as a teacher to enable as many children as possible to achieve their potential.

As another interviewee, also employed in a "caring" profession, observed, it is easy to see this kind of work as part of the PSW vocation, but interviewees whose work was not so obviously understood in this way also affirmed their sense of their secular work being part of their vocation. One interviewee, who summed up his work as being a bureaucrat, took pride in being good at his job, pleased that a line manager, in an annual appraisal, had said to him, "You didn't accept the call to be a priest in the church of God to be a bureaucrat, but it doesn't stop you being good at it." Later he reaffirmed that "for me it [being a priest] is the core and I happen to be a bureaucrat. But I think it's a good way at the moment of using my God-given skills".

Another interviewee emphasized: "You have to do a decent job of whatever it is you're being paid for." In her follow-up interview, she expressed very clearly "the feeling that your work is valuable to God" in and for itself. She saw an important part of what she does in the church as "valuing what everybody does; it's not just the work you do for the church, it's not for being the church treasurer, or running the Sunday School, or the coffee rota". In her first interview, she had talked about a person who ran the coffee rota seeing that as her service to God, but ignoring all that she did in her job as a hairdresser. This was not simply about chatting or listening to her clients, but that, by doing her work well, "she's making them feel better because they look a little bit better", which is "a hugely important service to other people"—as all of us who waited weeks for a haircut during the 2020 lockdowns can testify! The interviewee who worked in health and safety talked about the importance of what he did because "it looks after people's wellbeing", continuing that he was very thorough, and would not let things go. Later he talked about an occasion when:

> . . . they asked me to close their [IT] systems down—bring it down to auditable level. I had a few directors a bit upset with me, because I took lots of privileges away from them, but they accepted it in the end.

Without exception, the interviewees all saw their work as important in its contribution to people's wellbeing, and also for its own sake. As one put it, "if one suspects it doesn't matter, then you lose a grip on the importance of the whole of your work". He then questioned whether his faith made him better at his job than his secular colleagues, one of the questions considered in the four PSW narratives. He concluded that it would be arrogant to say that it did, and, of course, he would never know if he would have been worse at his job if he were not a priest, or a person of faith, and so: "I think the two eyes, where one says, yeah, it's important; and the other, no, it doesn't make me better, are both important to me."

The interviewees' view that their secular work mattered in and for itself, and that doing it well was an important way in which they realized their vocations, helps to confirm my feeling that work is a primary theological category. As Dorothy L. Sayers wrote, work is a way in which human nature finds "its proper exercise and delight and so fulfils itself to the glory of God",[282] or as *Laborem exercens*[283] put it: "human work is *a key*, probably *the essential key*" to making "life more human". Whether this is co-creation with God, as *Laborem exercens* claimed, or simply engagement with God in God's work (the *missio Dei*), does not appear to me to be the fundamental issue, which is that this world, all of it, is part of God's creation, and so part of what God wills to redeem.

Seeking God in the mess

Not all work can be called good work, however, and even work which is mostly good has its issues. Describing how she saw her vocation as different from that of the FTS, one of the interviewees said:

> I think it's partly because people who have spent most of their life in full-time parish-based ministry simply don't have the same experiences, which have been gained in contexts that they may have been somehow or other trained to regard as slightly iffy. I mean, all this management stuff and money, and decisions, and risk-taking and so on, and that's not what, that's not what you're about if you're a member of the clergy. That's messy stuff, somehow.

A little later she commented that:

> . . . there may be a feeling that secular management is nasty, and sacks people, and disciplines people, and things, and if we are—I caricature to a certain extent—but if we're nice, holy people, we don't behave in that sort of way, we have a different way of going about things.

Another interviewee expressed a sense of frustration:

> . . . that they [FTSs] compartmentalize their life a lot, and they don't recognize that the world is a bit more messy than it used to be. And for things like protected sabbath time, I'm in absolute agreement—in absolute agreement that we should all have a day off a week, and I accept that, and I think that's great—I wish I did every—but when you come across stumbling blocks, like, no, I can't do that, it's my day off . . .

Yet another interviewee described doing some work with a group of FTSs working in "some of the tough, outer estates around the cities of Britain" who are "fantastic, they're deeply interested in their parishes and the people, in the culture, and so on". He found, however, that "when we moved from reflection to action, something kind of drains out of the conversation". His point was that in his job he has to identify a problem, decide what is to be done about it, by whom, by when, and how "will we know we've done it?", and "so the work ethic is different".

As the excerpts above show, the interviewees felt that the FTS is to some extent protected from many of the issues with which the PSW has to grapple. Although one commented that it was "a bit of a doddle" to "join the dots" to see how one might seek God in professions such as teaching and counselling, dedicating one's "working life . . . to helping other people grow", he also talked about a PSW he had known who was a secretary to a small building firm: "Maybe a building site is a good place to spend time, but you have to discover why." Later, he mentioned an occasion when his wife, who was a schoolteacher at the time, was:

> . . . doing some work on the workplace, and she realized after a bit that there was a look of incomprehension, because she was actually reflecting on her own experience of working as a schoolteacher. But she'd got a class of kids, all of whose fathers were employed on the track at Chrysler, where the question why are you here, and there was only one answer, it pays better than anywhere else, but that it's no way to spend time really . . .

The alienation of work was an issue for another interviewee, specifically the situation of:

> . . . a guy who used to help me with the youth club, who was a machine operator, lathe operator. He said, "I've worked there for", I can't remember, thirty odd years. "I have never known what it is I am making. I simply make a part to the drawing, and I don't know what it is, or what it'll be used for."

The interviewee continued:

> . . . we had someone—we were very short of churchwardens, and someone who always came to church with his family said, "Do you have to be confirmed to be a churchwarden?", and well, yeah,

yes, you do, actually. He said, "Well, I can't do it then. I'd be very happy to be churchwarden, but if I got confirmed, I would have to take seriously the ethics of what I do in weapons research, Monday to Friday. And I have a mortgage to pay, and I have kids to support, and it's a question I dare not let myself ask . . . "

It was issues like these which led to his leaving full-time parish ministry to pursue a vocation as a PSW, because "it was about people's working lives, . . . it was work questions people were bringing into their engagement with the church, and we didn't know how to deal with them". Such questions resulted in his participation in research about the experience of people, who had gone into their professions believing them to be part of their Christian vocation. Sooner or later, they had run into problems, such as "bankers saying 'I thought my job was to manage money responsibly, and now I am simply there to sell financial products to people who often will be disadvantaged by buying them'". However, when people took these issues back to their church leaders, the responses fell into three categories: "One is, I'll pray for you; one is, why don't you get another job; and the other is blank incomprehension, that was the gamut of response from the ministers, the clergy." For him this was clear evidence of the failure of the church to connect with the very real problems which lay Christians encounter in their workplaces.

It is because work is not always good, because it too is affected by the Fall, that the workplace is the place the PSW is called to be:

> It was tough. And, in a way, I think one of the things I enjoyed about the [workplace], was working with the tough bits because that way we were working with the real, and, in some sense, that we can't be so precious about our place, that we have always to be pure . . . [we have to] be happy to get our hands dirty, or else who will?

For me, it is an article of faith that God cares for all creation, and so there can be no workplaces or workers who are beyond redemption. Volf's argument that human work matters, because it contributes to the eschatological building of God's kingdom, the *missio Dei*, is therefore one that appeals to me, and that is the context in which I see the secular work of the PSW. Our work matters to God, so it matters that we do it well, and that we find ways to engage with the messy issues that work and workplaces throw at us.

Accepting the cost

There can be a personal cost in being involved as a priest in a secular workplace. In general, the interviewees were content with their lot, finding "a lot of fulfilment and a great deal of joy" in doing what they do, but were prepared to accept that there might be a personal cost, which is inherent in taking discipleship seriously. One interviewee talked about having " . . . looked at other jobs, and thought my time is up, and God quite happily bangs me on the shoulders and says, 'No, you're still needed here'". He did not feel free to simply please himself, or to focus purely on career development, but rather that his employment was part of his vocation, and so part of what he had committed to God.

This story from one of the teachers illustrates the personal cost. She had taken two funerals for colleagues' husbands:

> One in particular was personally costly, because the widow is . . . in her mid- to late-thirties, two young children and her husband killed himself. And I knew him, because she was in my department, and so we mingled socially. And I didn't know him as a close friend, and we—and I, together, or I, I can't remember now[284]—but they came to us for the baptism of their younger child. And so there were former colleagues there who turned to me for support at the funeral, and I was supporting [the widow] and her children, and her parents and his parents. And because I also wanted to know why—where he killed himself was in his place of work, which was in our parish—why didn't he think he could come here? . . .
>
> Also, one time she wanted to talk to me, but turned up at church five minutes before the service started, and I spent half the service standing in the graveyard talking to her, because she knew where she'd find me at that time. So there was a personal cost in my sense of loss, and puzzlement about the finality and

> desperation of the situation. But the ongoing cost of [the widow's] very difficult journey, because, obviously, I'm walking with her on it . . .

In addition to supporting the widow, the parents, and work colleagues, there were also the two young children to consider, so she had planned a funeral which would include them:

> I've never done one like that before, and I had to make it up. And I think that is part of the challenge where people turn to me from my secular world of work, they don't know how church does things, but they want me to be church for them their way.

Almost all ministers will have had the experience of taking a difficult funeral and will know the personal cost in walking alongside the mourners; indeed, this is what funeral ministry is about. However, I think there is something qualitatively different about the ministry of the interviewee to her bereaved colleague, because their relationship as secular colleagues is different from the relationship between a priest and a parishioner, even if previously well known. The closest parallel I have come across is the funeral which an incumbent I know had to conduct for one of her churchwardens, who had also, over the years, become a personal friend, so similarly both colleague and friend.

Conclusion: Working with God in the *missio Dei*

As one of the interviewees put it:

> What gets me up in the morning? What gets me up is thinking that I can play my part in building God's kingdom here on earth, a bit, at the [workplace], or in the parish and that, for me, is a huge sense of joy and achievement. . . . that privilege of knowing that you are doing God's work is incredibly joyful and affirming . . . .

Like Andrew and his companion, we seek the Messiah; we seek to work with God. We work with God as best we can because that is what God has asked us to do, in part because it fulfils us and our sense of vocation, but also because, as priests, we work with others, enabling them to recognize this sense of calling for themselves. It's "all around the idea of *missio Dei*, really", because "ordinary people [need to be able to] see and feel that everything that they do is part of vocation, in inverted commas, or building the kingdom, or service to God, or whatever particular terms you want to use for it". Being part of the *missio Dei*, helping to build the kingdom, should be the *raison d'être* of any Christian; for the PSW, their involvement in secular work, together with their church-based ministry, is the context in which "we are required to help build God's kingdom here on earth, that's what it's about".

In this age, the *saeculum*, all is subject both to sin and to God's transforming work, the church no less than a factory or a weapons research establishment. If it were the case that this present age is to be annihilated at the Parousia, then nothing we do now is of any real significance. Jesus' incarnation is the evidence that God has not abandoned this world, however, and so Andrew's recognition that, in meeting Jesus, he had found the Messiah is the answer to "what do you seek?" We seek the Messiah, because we know at some level that we want to be part of Jerusalem, not Babylon, to be heirs of Christ rather than Adam: "Every human being is an heir of Adam and suffers the same alienation from self and from other persons and creatures—which also means estrangement from God," but by the grace of God, we can be heirs of Christ (Romans 5:12–21).[285]

PSWs seek the Messiah, doing what they can to embody God's transforming love through their work and their presence in the workplace, and through all that they do to contribute to the *missio Dei*. The PSW's commitment to their work, even though it is not perfect and there may be difficult ethical issues to be resolved, is one way of saying that what we do now does matter, that it is of significance: "Why or what we do may be of little worth in some ways, and we shouldn't insist that it's different from that. Nevertheless, it's as though it is of huge worth, if you see what I mean?"

CHAPTER 10

Where are you staying?

And John [the Baptist] testified, "I saw the Spirit descending from heaven like a dove, and it remained (*emeinen*) on him. I myself did not know him, but the one who sent me to baptize with water said to me, 'He on whom you see the Spirit descend and remain (*menon*) is the one who baptizes with the Holy Spirit.' And I myself have seen and have testified that this is the Son of God."

The next day John again was standing with two of his disciples, and as he watched Jesus walk by, he exclaimed, "Look, here is the Lamb of God!" The two disciples heard him say this, and they followed Jesus. . . . They said to him, "Rabbi" (which translated means Teacher), "where are you staying (*meneis*)?" He said to them, "Come and see." They came and saw where he was staying (*menei*), and they remained (*emeinan*) with him that day.

John 1:32–37,38b–39

The words translated "staying" and "remain(ed)" in this passage are forms of the Greek *menein*, which is preserved in the English "remain" and "maintain": *menein* is an important verb in John's Gospel, not least in Chapter 15, where it is generally translated "abide". When Andrew and his companion ask Jesus "where are you staying/abiding", therefore, the question operates on more than one level. They want to know the house in which Jesus is staying (currently), but this is also a question about where Jesus abides, implying an eternal focus. When Jesus tells them to come and see, and then they remain (*emeinan*) with him, they are being brought into the company of those who abide with Jesus. This story is thus not simply about the response of two individuals to Jesus, but recounts Jesus' calling into being the messianic community, formed of those who recognize him as Messiah, who will accompany him from that point onwards, and will abide with him in his eternal home, through the work of the Holy Spirit. The church is the post-Pentecost continuation of that messianic community, in which ordinary people become aware of the Messiah in their midst and, finding where he is, remain/abide with him.

Where do I stay?

In early work in this research, and in earlier drafts of this chapter, I focused on exile as a significant theme both in the Bible and in my own story. I entitled my first research paper "How shall we sing the Lord's song in a strange land? On being a minister in secular employment".[286] I find Psalm 137 evokes memories of dislocation for me, and the cry from the heart which formed the title of that paper is one I have wrestled with, particularly in the early years after my ordination, as I have described already.[287] I have come to see, however, that the resonance is not about exile, but about strange lands and finding that God is present there. I found Christopher Rowland's description of Babylon as both the place of exile, but also symbolic of the challenge of "being confronted by an alien set of values, cultural and political dislocation, and the necessity of negotiating a way of existing in that situation",[288] helpful in enabling me to make some sense of why the theme of exile still resonates for me, and why I still feel it needs a place here.

I have already mentioned the time when my children were small, and my then-husband's job took us to Arizona for almost six months. I arrived knowing no one but my own immediate family, needing to make many adjustments to life in a very different culture. It was indeed a strange land: something as simple as going shopping proved challenging, as I pushed my baby in her buggy, three more small children in tow, along a road without any pavements to the shopping mall I could clearly see, but could not work out how to enter. I had yet to discover that American cities are constructed on the premise that everyone drives everywhere, and because no one walks, there is no need for pavements/sidewalks or pedestrian routes. Key to settling in, so that the strange gradually became familiar, were the people I met: there was the young mother I met in the line for the immunization clinic;[289] there was the principal of the pre-school in which I enrolled my middle two children; and there were people from a nearby church who heard that there was a new family in the neighbourhood and called round to visit us.

As I think about that time, however, what is uppermost in my mind is the desert. Nothing in my previous experience had prepared me for its impact. We spent most weekends driving vast distances across the Arizona deserts to go to places like the Grand Canyon, the Painted Desert and the Petrified Forest. We went up into Utah to see the "Badlands" and into New Mexico, California and Nevada. The first time we went to the Grand Canyon, soon after our arrival, we left Phoenix in hot sunshine, the children in shorts and T-shirts. By the time we reached Flagstaff, less than three hours later but some 1800m higher, it was snowing and we had to stop to buy warm jumpers and trousers. Everything in Arizona was on a completely different scale from home: the colours, the extremes of temperature, the vast emptiness of the desert, the distances between one town and the next.

It was also more hostile than home. Before we had unpacked in our rented home, the man who sprayed everywhere to ensure that we were not troubled by poisonous spiders and scorpions arrived with his equipment, warning me to keep the mesh screens closed on windows and doors, and not to hang my laundry outside to dry, because I would bring it in full of insects, some of them better avoided. Out in the desert, one of my daughters discovered the hard way why some of the cacti were called "jumping cacti". A picnic was hastily curtailed when we were besieged by what looked like wasps but were twice the size.

The church we settled in was not the large First Baptist Church that we tried first, but a relatively small neighbourhood Southern Baptist congregation. Week by week, we went to Sunday School classes for an hour, and then into worship for an hour (at least). We heard altar call after altar call and listened to many personal testimonies (often repeated a week or two later). Theologically, we came from a very different tradition; yet the welcome was sincere, and the hospitality felt limitless. At Thanksgiving, we encountered a roast turkey dinner complete with jello salad, where small cubes of vegetables were encased in sweet green jelly, and in return, we introduced them to Christmas pudding and custard—I'm not sure who was more bemused or uncertain about what they were eating!

It was a formative time in my life, a time when I realized how big the world is, and how much there is to experience. It was a time when I realized that familial and societal restrictions on what the mother of small children could/should (not) do were not sacrosanct, and that not only was I perfectly capable of making my way in a new and very different environment, but I could make a success of it. It was a time when I indulged my desire to see more and to experience more, to test out all kinds of limits, taking my family with me, willing or otherwise. I fell in love with the desert extremes, with the colours, the landscapes, the amazing variety of plants squeezing life out of a hostile environment.

I also led us into potential disaster. One winter's day, we took our family-sized (but small by American standards) car, with ordinary tyres, up into a mountainous area where the roads were closed other than to four-wheel drive vehicles. The landscape was empty and phenomenally beautiful: slopes covered with drifting virgin snow blowing across yellowy-green grass tussocks as far as the eye could see, and blue, blue skies. And then the car skidded, leaving the road and landing up in the bushes, close to a sheer drop. My husband tried to reverse it back onto the road, without success. I was terrified that he would end up sliding over the edge. We were saved when a passing truck stopped, and the driver brought out his hauling ropes and pulled the car back to safety.

I am still attracted to empty places, and I still prefer to locate myself at the edges of the communities of which I am a part. A few years ago, leading worship for a small rural congregation, I preached a sermon based on the song "A Horse With No Name",[290] in which the line "I've been through the desert on a horse with no name" occurs several times. That sermon no longer exists on my computer, and I do not remember what my point was, other than that "In the desert you can remember your name". For me, "outside the camp" (cf. Hebrews 13:13–14) is the place where I feel free, where I feel my soul expanding, where I meet the God who calls me by that name,[291] the place where God abides with me, and I can know God's presence without all the distraction with which I am generally surrounded.

Theology of place

"To know who you are is to be oriented in moral space."[292] So wrote the Canadian philosopher Charles Taylor, by which he meant a space in which we work out the difference between "good or bad, what is worth doing and what not, what has meaning and importance . . . and what is trivial and secondary". For Taylor, our moral orientation is one way in which we answer questions about who we are, because we are framed by our commitments (such as Catholic or anarchist) and by our identifications (such as Armenian or Québécois), but "our identity is deeper and more many-sided than any of our possible articulations of it": "our identities define the space of qualitative distinctions within which we live and choose".[293] The place and the community in which we live contribute to our identities.

Space and place: *Dasein*
"Space" and "place" are not the same. Where "space" is "out there" and infinite, "place" is "in here", local, significant, and familiar: "Spaces are what are filled with places";[294] "When space feels thoroughly familiar to us, it has become place."[295] This underlies the philosopher Heidegger's concept of *Dasein*, often translated into English by the word "existence", but with a spatial nuance of "being there" or "presence", which "existence" does not really encompass. It is the word used by Heidegger for specifically human existence or being, and refers to "the inherently social being who . . . operates with a pre-theoretical grasp of the *a priori* structures that make possible particular modes of Being", which "realize some form of presence . . . to human beings".[296] *Dasein* dwells in the world in the way that we dwell in our homes, places which are familiar, where we belong: "It is in this sense that *Dasein* is (essentially) in the world." In his *A Christian Theology of Place*, Bishop John Inge claimed that Heidegger's *Dasein* is "rooted in time and space. Man *[sic]* is not a subject apart from the world . . . but an integral, immersed member".[297]

Interestingly, Heidegger linked *Dasein* with *Logos* (cf. John 1:1–14), through the concept of "being present".[298] Inge did not mention this, although he did focus on Heidegger's concept of "dwelling", linking it with the etymology of *bauen*, which in Old English and High German meant "to dwell", and which is now a German word for "building". *Dasein* thus embodies existence not as an abstract concept, but as a rooted human being, who dwells in a specific place at a specific time with other human beings: "place" is what gives Heidegger's *Dasein* its sense of rooted identity. In John 1:14, we are told that the *Logos* became flesh and dwelt among us: the incarnation is the supreme example of rooted identity, the second person of the Trinity made man and living a human life in a specific place at a specific time.

Place in the Bible

Place is a significant theme in the Pentateuch, from the expulsion of Adam and Eve from the Garden of Eden (Genesis 3), to Abram's journey from Ur of the Chaldees to become Abraham, the father of a great nation in the land of the promise in Canaan (Genesis 12–18); from the migration to Egypt (Genesis 37–50) to the exodus and wilderness period (the content of the other four books of the Pentateuch), followed by resettlement in the Promised Land (Numbers 34, cf. Joshua 2–12). The historical validity of these accounts is irrelevant to the argument here, which is that place is a key concept. This is reinforced in the accounts of the loss of first the land occupied by the ten tribes of the Northern Kingdom of Israel to the Assyrians in the mid eighth century BCE (2 Kings 15–18), followed by the loss of independence of the remaining two tribes of the Kingdom of Judah to Babylon in the early sixth century BCE (2 Kings 25); both of these resulted in a substantial proportion of the governing classes at least being taken into exile. Not surprisingly, the exodus, wilderness wanderings and the exile are highly significant in the biblical narrative, but the periods of settlement in the land were not without their problems either.[299] It is disconcerting for the twenty-first-century reader of 1 Kings to discover that Solomon built the temple, and much else, using slave labour (1 Kings 9:15–23). In Nehemiah's account of the return to the land, the author lamented that Israel was still not independent, with foreign rulers having "power also over our bodies and over our livestock at their pleasure" (Nehemiah 9:36–37).

In the Hebrew scriptures, Yahweh was the God who went with Israel in the wilderness, actualized in the ark of the covenant, and was the God of the Promised Land, actualized by Yahweh's presence in the temple. The fall of Jerusalem in 587 or 586 BCE, with the loss of the temple, meant that Israel had to wrestle with what that meant in terms of Yahweh's presence with them (cf. Psalm 137). For the early Christians, that question was answered in the person of Jesus Christ (e.g. Mark 13; John 2:18–22), whose one complete sacrifice rendered void the Hebrew sacrificial system (e.g. Hebrews 10:1–18). The incarnation affirmed the significance of the particular in both place and time, but Jerusalem remained a potent eschatological symbol (Revelation 21; Hebrews 12:22–24), and place was still significant (e.g. John 14:1–6).[300] This is exemplified by the explicit geographical locations provided for key events, such as the disciples' meeting with the risen Lord on the road to Emmaus (Luke 24:13–35), and St Paul's dramatic conversion on the road to Damascus (Acts 9:3–9).

Sacred space

For modern urban dwellers, the concept of "place" has become problematic. When every town centre has the same stores, and every shopping mall and McDonald's restaurant looks the same, place loses its particularity, and begins to revert to undifferentiated space.[301] The loss of distinctive space in our towns and cities, rapid travel, and instantaneous 24/7 global news, have all contributed to changing what "local" means, as has the irrelevance of locality on the internet. We see this played out globally in the difficulties governments experience in trying to tax multinational giants such as Amazon and Google.[302]

There are resonances here with Eliade's distinction between sacred space, which is oriented and heterogeneous, and profane space, which is amorphous and chaotic (Chapter 2).[303] Perhaps a sense of lack of "locatedness" is one explanation for the proliferation of roadside memorials in recent years, marking the spot where a fatality occurred. This may also in part explain the popularity of forms of spirituality which emphasize "thin places", which are deemed particularly sacred.[304] Inge, therefore, asked whether some places are more likely to be places where God reveals Godself, or to be boundary places "between the material world and the other world".[305] His answer was that it is not that some places are intrinsically more likely to be places of revelation, but that, conversely, the revelation of God, or an experience of God, could lead to some places being deemed sacred.

This begs the question, however, as to what we mean by "sacred space" or a "sacred place". Eliade's concept of profane space as without orientation and chaotic derives from his argument that primitive societies believed that outside the known world was chaos.[306] The ritual of taking a land, as exemplified in the biblical account of ancient Israel's arrival in the Promised Land, or by fifteenth- and sixteenth-century Christians from Spain and Portugal in the Americas, is therefore highly significant, which Eliade sees as taking what was profane and enabling it to become sacred.[307] Once a space becomes sacred, it can operate as a point of communication between earth and heaven, like Jacob's ladder; ground becomes holy when it provides a way to reach heaven.

Narratives like these, however, ignore the contested nature of sacred space: contemporary Jerusalem is a prime example of this.[308] Similarly, in the light of the Black Lives Matter movement,[309] the conquest of the Americas is better understood as a story of exploitation of, and atrocity against, the indigenous peoples. European invaders took sacred sites in the Americas with little consideration that they might be committing sacrilege in the eyes of the people already living there. While such groups are not a single entity, but consist of many tribes, with different customs and attitudes to current white settlement, Native Americans agree about "a history of trauma and oppression, explicit and premeditated genocide followed by cultural genocide, resource appropriation, and broken agreements".[310] In her analysis of the origins of alternative spiritualities in the USA, Crockford described how Sedona, Arizona, was considered sacred by the Yavapai, a Native American tribe "who occupied the land and were forcibly removed by the American army to make space for the white settlers who came from the late nineteenth century". The Yavapai, who still live in the area, "are concerned they will not be able to access the land for ritual use" because of development brought about by white Americans seeking spiritual experience, and the resulting tourist industry. Sacred space is thus not a simple concept: a space may be considered sacred by different people for different reasons, perhaps resulting in conflict over the space.

There is also a tension between seeing somewhere as holy, perhaps because of its association with a particular holy person or an experience of God's self-revelation, and remembering that God is not to be confined or bounded, and is always free to act somewhere else.[311] As the angel said to Mary Magdalene and the other Mary on the day of resurrection, "He is not here . . . tell his disciples, '. . . he is going ahead of you'" (Matthew 28:6-7). Because in Christian belief, the sacred is located fundamentally in Jesus, place *per se* is less significant than the experience of God that occurs there.[312]

Interviewees' perspectives

In Mark's Gospel, Jesus is frequently to be found in marginal places in the wilderness (e.g. Mark 1) and around the Sea of Galilee (e.g. Mark 7:31). E. S. Malbon has argued that the Sea of Galilee "is the geographical focal point for the first half of the Gospel of Mark, the center *[sic]* of the Marcan Jesus' movement in space".[313] Crossing the Sea of Galilee puts Jesus between Jewish and Gentile territory: it is a liminal place. The Sea is not a barrier to him,[314] but is the place where he demonstrates his power over the elements, symbolized by the water as the realm of chaos, compared to the land as the place of promise, and yet it is, like the land, a place in which he demonstrates God's kingdom coming into effect.

That sense of being in a liminal place, or a place of ambiguity, came out again and again in the interviews.

Living in the ambiguity

> It's actually living in that ambiguity that's at the heart of what living as a Christian is about, and so the search for erasing ambiguity from structures of ministry is fated to fail.

The interviewee defined this ambiguity as "living in the theological interim between Pentecost and the Parousia", in which we "live with the grace of the Holy Spirit, and we live with the persistence of sin". In this age, there is no possibility of perfect Christian living; inevitably we will fail, because of the reality of sin. That means there is also no possibility of finding a perfect structure of ministry for the church: the church and its ministry are also under both sin and grace, and so are just as much in need of the redemptive activity of God. For the interviewee, this is the reason that we need an ordained priesthood:

> We are a priesthood of all believers, but because of our sinful natures we can't do that ultimately collective thing, and we have to have some who are set apart to do it in a very focused way, and in public.

Following Augustine, R. A. Markus discussed how this is the age of the gospel and the church, the age in which humans "are reformed in the image of God".[315] There will be no final separation of what is redeemable and what is not until the final judgement, and for that reason, this age is inherently provisional and ambiguous in its nature.[316] The church and the world are inseparable, both part of what is sacred, because redeemable, and part of what is profane. As Bonhoeffer argued, the vocation of the church is to witness to that redemption. Perhaps understanding and affirming the presence of PSWs in workplaces is one way in which the Church of England could so witness.

Standing on the threshold
In one of the follow-up interviews, I asked the interviewee if there was anything she wanted to add to what we had already discussed. She responded:

> There is one thing I'd like to add that I probably didn't communicate, which is, it's wonderful, a wonderful role, if you're the right person. If you don't mind being outside the city gates, or just standing on the threshold with your head swivelling both ways in and out.

The ambiguity discussed above means that there is no "pure" church already destined for redemption, any more than any part of the world outside the church is inevitably destined for annihilation. The parable of the wheat and the tares, referenced by Augustine in his characterization of the relationship between church and world, asserts that there can be no clear boundary between the church and the world.[317] Being outside the city gates, standing on the threshold, are metaphors which express the place that all priests need to occupy vis-à-vis church and world. They do, of course—no priest lives entirely within the confines of the institutional church—but the particular vocation of the PSW ensures that this issue is fore-grounded.

The admission in the original preamble for *Setting God's People Free*, that the Church of England has been much stronger at freeing and equipping God's people to serve Christ in church-based ministries than in their Monday to Saturday daily lives, suggests that the church has not encouraged people to go to the margins, to look out as well as in. The current report admits that the "needs and perspectives of lay people are not well heard, listened to, understood or acted on. As a result the Church of England is nowhere near as effective as it might be in equipping lay people effectively for mission in the whole of life."[318] One interviewee, talking about the difficulty in providing resources which actually help people in this, speculated that "those trying to respond are so trammelled by the way the church does things, that it can't actually equip people for a very 'unchurch-y' context". His claim, that there is an "existential gap between discipleship and being a worker", suggests that he does not think the church, in its institutional form, is in fact able to equip people "to follow Jesus confidently in every sphere of life".[319]

Being connected

> This is what you do; this is how priesthood is connected; it's connected with the South African dockers and the English dockers, even though they don't care about each other.[320] And so it's all, all—for me, it was about people at work, it wasn't about a sector of ministry it was about the life of the people, from the people in the weapons research station through to the dockers, and the shop workers.

This interviewee was explaining to me why he had decided to leave parish ministry to focus on ministry amongst people at work. His explanation took us through many stories about the working lives of people he had known, which had contributed to his decision. In the midst of these stories, he made that brief remark—that "this is how priesthood is connected". I described earlier in this book how I happened to look through a book on NSM in the 1970s, and that, in my memory, I read something about the difficulty the NSMs experienced in trying to hold the tension of being simultaneously in secular work and in parish ministry. As I explained there, this comment is not in fact in the book, but nevertheless has proved seminal for me throughout this research. Holding the tension, it seems to me, is how priests connect people and things which would not otherwise be connected. For the PSW, it is about connecting the church and the secular workplace, "it's about being seen as a person who is the church throughout the week", who bridges "the existential gap between discipleship and being a worker", so enabling "the everyday, the quotidian [to become] sacred".

The interviewee argued that there is a gap in language between the church and the workplace,[321] however, illustrating his point with a story about the Sheffield Industrial Missioners going into the steelworks in the post-war period, but being unable to bridge the gap between the church and the steelworkers. For him, this is an example of the need for "constant translation and iteration of theological language and secular language". He went on to talk about needing to speak Creole "where you can be understood by both [Pidgin speakers and home language speakers] simultaneously, although you're not speaking either fluently, totally fluently". A little later, he expanded on this, saying:

> . . . it's not just translation, we have to find the language that can encompass all of them, even though you might skew it slightly differently for different audiences. If it were just translation, you could challenge the nature of the translation: is this really that? But if you can talk the Creole . . . you can be understood.

This raises an interesting point about the need to be understood in a way that does not open us to challenge because our translation is inexact, but is comprehensible on all levels.

He also told the story of the French worker priest who went to work for Euro Disney, because his bishop was concerned about the welfare of the Euro Disney employees.[322] The priest "insisted, he held out to drive the train", because "that got him round the site and he could talk unaccompanied with other workers". He also "made an alliance with the local parish priest" so that he could create "a safe haven in a local parish church outside the Euro Disney site".

Another story concerned a railway chaplain he had known:

> . . . he knew that a gang of platelayers got together for tea in this dirty old cabin miles down a line, and he'd wander down the trackside and go and sit with them. Month after month they'd cut him dead, and didn't—wouldn't speak to him, wouldn't respond, and he just sat and went there faithfully every month until someone turned to him and said, "You must have a hide like a fucking rhino!" and the ice was broken . . .

The point of these stories was to illustrate how priests can make connections, how they can learn to speak the Creole, which enables them to be church for people who would not otherwise encounter the church. It requires them to hold the tension between contexts which are existentially quite separate, "to straddle the gap" and allow people to "walk over you".

Aware of God in all of life

A major theme in the Hebrew scriptures is the tension the people felt between knowing God was with them, symbolized in the ark of the covenant in the wilderness years, and then in the temple, and having to discover where God is when the temple is destroyed, and the people are in exile ("How could we sing the Lord's song in a foreign land?", Psalm 137:4). Because the place of exile is not the place of belonging, it is a place where God has to be sought, where God's presence cannot be taken for granted.[323] In the earlier discussion of what makes a particular place sacred, I quoted Etty Hillesum's account of finding a sacred place in her bathroom.[324] A bathroom is not sacred in itself, but because Hillesum found herself kneeling there in prayer, it became so. Places become sacred for people because God has revealed Godself there, or at least there is a sense of transcendence, of being on holy ground, of knowing that God is present (e.g. the burning bush and Jacob's ladder).

The PSW lives with ambiguity, on the threshold between the church and the workplace, connecting people and things which are not otherwise connected. To do this requires recognizing that their vocation is one, and that it is to be aware of God in all of life, and to find ways to witness to God's presence, even if explicit words would not be permissible.[325] One interviewee talked about "being a presence, of bringing the church into the community in a very tangible way", by which he meant that because he was a priest, he brought the church with him "meeting people where they're at". For another, it was being "like St Paul . . . out and about, part of the community", which meant that "I am you, I am part of you".

One interviewee told a story about an ordinand he had known, who worked on the railways, who said, "I want to know what it means to be a priest on the line side", to which the interviewee replied, "'You'll only find out by doing it, so get on with it.' . . . I think he thought there was an answer: you do this and you don't do that, but he learnt it wasn't like that at all." We find out what it means to be priests in whatever our contexts are through being "committed to contemplation that others may not be, [recognizing] that the contemplation is not essential, but is perhaps sufficient to the expression of God". The contemplation of God in the workplace then enables the PSW to see God's work there, or as one interviewee put it, to see how "the gifts of the Spirit can be worked out in the secular world".

Conclusion: sacramental presence

Earlier in this chapter, I referred to a remark by one of the interviewees, that the task of the PSW is to straddle the existential gap between discipleship and working life. In retrospect, I wish I had asked him to say a bit more about this, because, for me, the PSW is a sacramental presence, part of how God intends this gap to be straddled.[326] The PSW is called to places which are "outside the camp", but these are the places of vocation, places where the church is called to witness to God's love for all of creation.

John 14–17 contains Jesus' farewell discourse, with John 15 including the well-known allegory of the vine, in which Jesus is the vine, the disciples are the branches, and the Father is the vine-grower. Abiding in Jesus, and having Jesus abide in the believer, as the branches are part of the vine, is a key theme of this Gospel, realized through Jesus' sacrificial love. In his meditation on this chapter, Jean Vanier wrote:

> The Word became flesh
> in order to lead us into communion with God.
> He came to bridge the gap
> that separates weak and vulnerable human beings from God. . . .
> But he came not only to dwell in us
> but also to act in and through us,
> to give life to others, in and through us.
> We are called to participate in the creative and loving activity of God.
> We will bear much fruit if we dwell in God.[327]

As the PSW abides in God, so God abides in the PSW, and so the PSW, called to work with God in the *missio Dei*, is enabled to be a means by which God can act in the world: in so doing, the PSW is a sacramental presence.

This is illustrated by this excerpt from an interview with one of the teachers, describing a ritual she had devised:

> . . . their last Year 11 lesson before they took their exams . . . I told them this would be happening, I gave them a little speech, and it was always about how important they were, how valuable they were as individuals, to take care of themselves in all respects. And I would then open the door and wait for the bell, and shake their hands and say "God bless you" as they left, and give them eye contact.

For her students, this was the point at which they effectively left school, even though they would return to take their exams, and might go on to another school for post-sixteen education. It is a key moment in life, acknowledged as such by the way that the interviewee handled it, and also acknowledged as a point at which she could convey to them their worth in God's eyes, through both her words and her eye contact, and in the blessing that she gave them.

She also told a story about an incident involving sacramental forgiveness:

> ... my department was a string of English classrooms along the thin corridor which was the main access to the PE department. And I developed a really good relationship with PE staff, particularly the blokes, who just thought I was off another, from another planet. And, to me, they were as well, but we met in the middle somewhere in space, and teased each other very happily. And they played a lot of practical jokes on me, but I used words to get my own back.
>
> But there was one man who had had a bit of time off, and they'd lost a baby—he and his wife—and one break time, loads of kids milling about, and he just came to . . . he was inside one of my English classrooms, and I was in the corridor and he came to the doorway and started to talk to me. And it was evident from the start this wasn't one of our jokey conversations, but he obviously felt he could trust me as a person and as a priest. And he told me that he and his wife had had an abortion, because something had gone wrong with the baby. I think—I think I remember this correctly, it was going to be Down's syndrome, and they didn't feel that they were equipped to bring up such a child.
>
> He was obviously struggling with this; he was guilty, and he had tears in his eyes, and he . . . The way the conversation went, in the end, I can honestly say it was an absolution, but not in the form that any priest would identify.
>
> < No purple stole?>
>
> No, and anyway I'm not high church, and I wouldn't know how to give a formal absolution. But I told him that he and his wife—because he was speaking for both of them, really, I said, "I don't judge you; you shouldn't judge yourselves, but you do need to forgive yourselves, it appears to me." And, at that point, he just threw his arms around me and buried his face in my neck for a little while, kids still milling about us. And it was just a moment

out of time, and it was a precious moment, and a very exhausting moment. I can honestly say that ministering for an hour is a lot more tiring than teaching a full timetable for a day.

< Because? >

It takes—because teaching comes from the heart and the mind . . . and sometimes the soul . . . but ministering is connecting with the whole spiritual world and it enters a different plane, and it's to do with eternity.

What the PSW provided for her colleague in that moment had nothing to do with his faith, or lack of it, but everything to do with her providing a place in which he could begin the process of healing from the traumatic effects of aborting a wanted baby. In the encounter, God could create through her a place of absolution and healing. Her being there, being who she was, became sacramental presence for that PE teacher, which she described as "to do with eternity". For me, this is a perfect illustration of Fiddes' claim that when "pastors speak the words, 'You are forgiven, go in peace', they are participating in the rhythm of God's forgiveness . . . making incarnate in their own flesh and blood the forgiving offer of God".[328]

Since completing my doctoral research project, I have been asked what part worship and the Eucharist play for the PSW. For myself, I know that being part of a worshipping community ensures that I stay consciously connected with the body of Christ. The experience of the first 2020 lockdown, when churches were closed and we could not meet as we normally would, made me aware of how much I missed being physically present in worship, especially the Eucharist. I find that interesting, given that I spent ten years of my professional life teaching through videoconference technology!

I found that some forms of so-called "virtual" worship worked better than others—I qualify "virtual" because the worship is hopefully real regardless of the medium in which it is conducted. I rapidly came to enjoy Morning and Evening Prayer by Zoom book-ending my working day, and then releasing me to go out for my daily walk. The Zoom services were more participatory and informal than had previously been the case. A question had been raised earlier in the year about the logic of holding

Environment Vigils in a church heated and lighted for the occasion, so the transfer to Zoom made good sense. The format needed adaptation, but my ten years of teaching by videoconference helped with that.

What I found increasingly difficult were the live-streamed Eucharists. In contrast to the Zoom services, I found them alienating, feeling like an onlooker rather than a participant. That is attributable to the difference in technology—in the case of the Zoom services, we could all see who else was there on screen, and anyone could be asked to contribute directly, unlike the live-streamed services. For me, the idea of a "spiritual communion" simply does not make sense: I did not feel that I was truly with the body of Christ, part of the celebration around Christ's table. I do not think it was about the absence of the bread and wine—indeed, I could have done as others did and supplied my own—it was more about the absence of the body of Christ, and that sense of sharing a celebration together at the same time, in the presence of each other.[329] Initially, when it was suggested that I could take my place on the rota to preside at such a Eucharist, I agreed, but the more I thought about it, the more uncomfortable I felt. In the end, I decided that if Christ's people in general had to fast from the Eucharist, then so would I.

When worship in churches resumed, it felt right even with the differences, which included the suspension of the common cup so that only the celebrant was able to receive the wine. For me, the thing that really mattered was that we, the body of Christ, were present and anyone who wanted could, in theory, be present within the limits of the number allowed in the building at any one time. I am comfortable with my current mixed economy of Zoom for non-Eucharistic services when that suits me better, and physical presence when I can, and in particular for the Eucharist.

Not wanting to rely simply on my own feelings and views, I talked to PSWs, including some of my original interviewees, about worship and the Eucharist. One interviewee said:

> I think that receiving communion and celebrating it (as an SSM I don't celebrate every Sunday) are the anchor of both my faith and my adherence to the rites of the Church of England. It keeps me rooted in the parish and keeps Jesus' sacrifice rooted in my

heart, strengthening me to keep going vocationally, whichever context I am in.

Another said that not only is the Eucharist important to him, but that it has acquired fresh impetus, explaining it through the concept of "Givenness":

> Imagine looking at a fine painting. Now just gaze. Do not reason or articulate. Allow the painting to develop a voice of its own. That is givenness. All thinking/hermeneutics is subsequent to that. I find this a useful idea in so much.
>
> So, as a PSW, so much of my work was what you might call "clinical". That is, there was behind it theories . . . Now the problem with theory is that it stops you seeing what is outside of the theory. So just gaze! What might that mean? It means that if I gaze at a client . . . I have half a chance of intuiting something to do with the presence of God in the outside, secular world. And, yes, I cannot distinguish this from a vain imagining in the first instance. But finding the divine in the secular is surely key to PSWs.
>
> Now if I gaze in a similar way at what is "given" through the Eucharist then I get a cross-feeding between the two experiences, sometimes. It is intuitive and beyond the strictly reasoned. But it is how the divine and the secular, at least in part, may feed each other.

He went on to talk about a new perception of what it means to sit at table with Jesus, who throughout that last supper knew that he was going to go out and die voluntarily. We are not alone in the worst that can happen to us.

Something that came up frequently was discussion of what it means to be in community, and how activities we do together cement community. Food is central to that, and so the Eucharistic celebration in which we give thanks to God for all God's gifts through the remembering of the last supper forms us as the body of Christ. So many rites of passage and important occasions are marked with a meal, after all. One PSW talked of feeling that a focus on the elements of bread and wine is to miss the point, which is that the "this" that Jesus tells us to do is the act of sharing, which resonates then with what we are doing during the Peace and in the Dismissal ("Go in peace, to love and serve the Lord").

Another PSW picked up on the dimension of sharing:

> For me my priestly ministry at work definitely has a Eucharistic dimension (as well as a kingly, prophetic, healing, etc. etc.). For me, this Eucharistic dimension mainly plays out in having lunch with colleagues from my research group. I share other meals with my colleagues such as teas (with cake), drinks (sometimes involving cheesy chips) after work, etc. But lunch because it is more "often" as in "do this as often as you eat this bread and drink this cup" is more important than these other more celebratory shared meals (although they too perhaps are foretastes of the Messianic Banquet). These everyday lunches are also "open to all" as we make a point of inviting everyone in the group to it.
>
> The best Eucharistic lunch we had recently (pre-lockdown) was the Monday after a farewell meal for a colleague, held at another colleague's house the day before. We'd all made and brought food for this meal on Sunday, so the lunch in the workplace canteen on Monday was of the leftovers which we shared (instead of buying or bringing our own individual food as we would normally have done). The food tasted delicious. We had all contributed to the making (the creating) of it. We were eating food up that would otherwise have been wasted (the saving of it). We were sharing more than physical food but memories too. We were thus joining in with the creating and saving work of God.
>
> The pandemic has interrupted these Eucharistic meals at work just as it has interrupted Eucharistic meals held in church buildings.

Then there was a conversation with yet another PSW about "secular sacraments". His starting point was the question which has motivated him over many years: "What does it mean to be a priest when you don't have an altar to cling onto?" Answering that, he talked about rites of passage, and the resonances between baptism/entering a new workplace, marriage/bringing together different teams or companies, death and serious illness/retirement and redundancy. These are important, because "if those things that we do in church have any meaning they should be translatable to the workplace". The occasional offices still have meaning for people because they help to mark the important rites of passage of ordinary life, as they have done over the centuries. We now live in many different "villages", but these rites are still important ways that we mark key moments in them, not least in the "village" of the workplace.

For this PSW, it is John the Baptist who makes sense of what it means to be a PSW. We too need to see where people are doing good/godly things and point to them, acknowledging them implicitly at least as being not far from the kingdom of God. In the workplace, absolution, blessing and celebration all happen, albeit not named in theological categories. Sometimes the role of the PSW is simply to notice, sometimes to encourage, sometimes it may be to take the lead, but always it is about recognizing God at work. It is our experience in worship, and particularly in the Eucharist, and our theological training and ministerial formation, which enable us to do this.

I admit to feeling some reservations about some of this, particularly where the Eucharist is concerned. When I first heard about the concept of, for instance, Friday lunch with work colleagues being in some sense sacramental, I felt this was absolutely a step too far. Discussing it more recently, I see the force of the argument, that God is not constrained by the practices of the church, and that God's grace is always available everywhere. On the other hand, that feeling of alienation caused by watching my colleagues celebrate the Eucharist on YouTube, when none of us were able to meet together in church, suggests to me that Stanley Hauerwas' and Samuel Wells' emphasis on the shared meal which binds Christians together is a significant counter argument.[330]

So finally, as one interviewee said: "I think we do finally stand with Christ, and not in the place of Christ, in his and our facing of the world." This is sacramental presence, because it mediates God's love, enabling it to be experienced, whether or not the recipient recognizes it as God's love. The vocation of the PSW is to be a public believer, given authority by the church to act in its name, and to be a sacramental presence, someone in whom Christ abides as they abide in Christ.

Postscript

I started this research because of the tension I personally experienced in holding together my new-found vocation to be a priest in the church of Christ, and my pre-existing vocation as a teacher and educator. I wanted to understand the nature of this vocation which embraces both ministry in the Church of England and engagement in secular work, both for my own personal satisfaction, but also in order to be able to say to the Church of England: this is who we are, this is why we matter. We are people who, by virtue of our ordination, have nailed our colours to the church's mast, and more specifically to that of the Church of England. We are also people who interpret God's call on our lives to mean that we work out our vocation as much through our secular work as in the church: on the one hand, our secular work matters to us as part of our call to serve God in God's world, and on the other, in being who we are in our given context, we embody God's presence in that place.

As mentioned in Chapter 3, in 2013 there was a celebration of self-supporting ministry in Southwark Cathedral on the fiftieth anniversary of the Southwark Ordination Course, which was the first course designed to train ordinands who wished or needed to remain in secular employment at least until ordination. The SSM representatives who attended described the blessings they experienced through being SSM and the problems they encountered. The participants in my research concurred with their comments about the richness of their experience, the opportunities to engage with people outside the boundaries of the institutional church, and their sense of freedom from some at least of the institutional limitations placed upon FTSs, as the quotations from the interviews in previous chapters confirm. They also felt that their gifts are not used to the full by the church, feeling that the church tries to squeeze them into the shape of a parochial minister and ignores what is not within its immediate scope.

Not much seemed to happen immediately, but I feel there is a gathering momentum, passing from Teresa Morgan's 2011 report, through the Southwark 2013 celebration, to John Lees' book on SSM in 2018, to the establishment of regular meetings of the national group of SSM advisers and others in 2020. Lees' book built on Morgan's survey, and was a recognition that "a flurry of writing about non-stipendiary clergy and worker priests" some four decades ago was not followed up until Francis and Francis' "seminal" volume, *Tentmaking: Perspectives on Self-supporting Ministry* in 1998, which was already becoming dated.[331] In the two and a half years that have passed since the publication of Lees' book, a group of SSM officers in the West Country has coalesced with a similar group in the eastern dioceses, and with others is now a national group. After the second eastern regional meeting, I wrote a report published in the *Church Times* which, among other things, called for a bishop to represent SSMs: that did happen, although the bishop appointed retired not long after.[332] With the consecration of Dame Sarah Mullally, a former nurse and Chief Nursing Officer, in 2015, there was at last a diocesan bishop in the Church of England who had been an SSM, in fact a PSW. CHRISM continues to attract a number of SSMs and others who self-identify as MSEs, and is now (September 2020) embarking on a theological discussion group. It has also published a number of papers and case studies about MSE: in 2019, an article on worker priests appeared in the *Church Times*.[333]

A real impetus has come about through the COVID-19 lockdown which started in March 2020, and resulted in a huge upsurge in the use of videoconferencing for meetings and events. The national group of SSMs is discussing what good and bad practice look like, and sharing some of the research that is now going on. This includes a project under the auspices of the Ministry Division of the Church of England on SSM, including PSWs within that. In fact, it is my belief that none of this is coincidental, that the Holy Spirit is at work and that SSM and PSW are ministries whose time has come.

My conclusion, formed through the research that I have undertaken across several years, and involving in total some fifty PSWs, is that the key concepts for understanding the unique vocation of those of us who are Church of England priests, engaged in secular work, are our identity as priests, the importance of our secular work as part of how we serve God, and our sense that we embody sacramental presence. My research question, in the end, was:

> How do people who are simultaneously ordained, licensed, priests in the Church of England and engaged in secular work make sense of their particular vocation?

In deciding that this was the question I wanted to answer, I also realized that the label for us which best sums up our sense of who we are is "priest in secular work", with the acronym PSW.

The PSW is called to be someone through whom God can act, fulfilling the priestly task of offering to God the joy, the ordinary and the mess that they encounter in the workplace and through their work, expressed so well by the interviewee who said:

> I'm ordained because that's what I felt called to be. It is ontological for me; it's not about status in the community or status in the congregation. It's, I suppose, reduce it to the sacrament of offering up daily life for myself and for others, in the Eucharist—not always at an altar—but in, so to speak, Eucharistic moments when the everyday, the quotidian becomes sacred. So that's always been at the heart of my theology of priesthood.

Understanding this as God's call on their lives gives PSWs a sense of fulfilment and joy:

> I hope somehow or other it came over . . . I mean, I do feel I do get a lot of fulfilment and a great deal of joy from doing what I do, and I don't know whether that comes across quite as strongly as I would like it to. I realized after I talked to you and you went away, and I was thinking about it later in the evening and I thought, yes, I really do . . . this is really important, it is really . . . I get a great deal out of doing this, and I enjoy doing it.

Each of us is one person, occupying a small part of the world for a finite period of time, but:

> I have an image of myself about one of the gifts of God, if one is a believer, which is that he *[sic]* requires us to write our lives across the sky. By which I think I mean that why or what we do may be of little worth in some ways, and we shouldn't insist that it's different from that. Nevertheless, it's as though it is of huge worth, if you see what I mean?

I have found great riches in my data, demonstrated by these three excerpts. In reflecting on them, I am reminded of a passage from Teilhard de Chardin, which has resonated for me since I first read it many years ago:

> Since once again, Lord—though not this time in the forests of the Aisne but in the steppes of Asia—I have neither bread, nor wine, nor altar, I will raise myself beyond these symbols, up to the pure majesty of the real itself; I, your priest, will make the whole earth my altar and on it will offer you all the labours and sufferings of the world.
>
> . . .
>
> My paten and my chalice are the depths of a soul laid widely open to all the forces which in a moment will rise up from every corner of the earth and converge upon the Spirit. Grant me the remembrance and the mystic presence of all those whom the light is now awakening to the new day.[334]

The PSW offers to God all that they find in their workplaces and in their encounters in the world, secular and sacred. Being called to be a PSW is demanding and yet a great privilege. As Gerard Manley Hopkins wrote in his poem "As Kingfishers Catch Fire":

> . . . *myself* it speaks and spells,
> Crying Whát I dó is me: for that I came.
> . . .

> Christ — for Christ plays in ten thousand places,
> Lovely in limbs, and lovely in eyes not his
> To the Father through the features of men's faces.[335]

Early in this research, I asked myself "who am I?", "what am I for?" We considered these questions in the co-operative inquiry group, and they informed the interviews. The answer is that we are PSWs, not simply non-stipendiary or self-supporting priests, but priests in secular work, and this is our vocation: to be bridges, to hold the tension, to live on thresholds and in ambiguity, to exercise ministry in the gaps, seeking out God in God's world and in God's people as we do our work to God's glory, making God explicit wherever we go. We seek Christ in "ten thousand places", and for this we are here.

Bibliography

Adams, I., *Wilderness Taunts* (Norwich: Canterbury Press, 2016).
Allen, R., *Missionary Methods: St Paul's or Ours?* (Grand Rapids, MI: Wm B Eerdmans Publishing Co, 1962).
Anderson, H. & Foley, E., "The Power of Storytelling", in Graham, E., Walton, H. & Ward, F. (eds), *Theological Reflection: Sources* (London: SCM Press, 2007), pp. 127–38.
Appiah, K. A., "Identity, Authenticity, Survival: Multicultural Societies and Social Reproduction", in Gutmann, A. (ed.), *Multiculturalism: Examining the Politics of Recognition* (Princeton, USA, and Chichester, UK: Princeton University Press, 1994), pp. 149–63.
Appiah, K. A., *The Ethics of Identity* (Princeton, NJ: Princeton University Press, 2005).
Aquinas, T., *Summa Theologiae*, <https://www.newadvent.org/summa/>, accessed 25 September 2020.
Archbishops' Council, *Setting God's People Free*, (GS 2056), <https://www.churchofengland.org/sites/default/files/2017-11/gs-2056-setting-gods-people-free.pdf>, (2017), accessed 23 September 2020.
Archbishops' Council, *Common Worship: Ordination Services* (London: Church House Publishing, 2007).
Archbishops' Council, *The Mission and Ministry of the Whole Church: Biblical, Theological and Contemporary Perspectives*, <https://www.churchofengland.org/sites/default/files/2018-01/The%20Mission%20and%20Ministry%20of%20the%20Whole%20Church.pdf>, (2007), accessed 25 September 2020.
Archbishops' Council, *No ordinary ministry: Ministers in secular employment*, <https://www.churchofengland.org/life-events/vocations/no-ordinary-ministry>, accessed 25 September 2020.
Archbishops' Council, *Setting God's People Free*, <https://www.churchofengland.org/SGPF>, (2017), accessed 25 September 2020.

Archbishops' Council, *Canons of the Church of England*, <https://www.churchofengland.org/more/policy-and-thinking/canons-church-england>, (2019), accessed 25 September 2020.
Augustine, *Confessions* (Harmondsworth: Penguin Books Ltd, 1961).
Augustine, *De Trinitate*, V, <https://www.newadvent.org/fathers/1301.htm>, (2020), accessed 25 September 2020.
Baker, J., *Blog*, <https://jonnybaker.blogs.com/>, accessed December 2020.
Baker, J., *Curating Worship* (London: SPCK, 2010).
Baptist Union of Great Britain, *In honour of Paul Fiddes*, <https://www.baptist.org.uk/Articles/422595/In_honour_of.aspx> (2014), accessed 25 September 2020.
Bennett, Z. & Rowland, C., *In a Glass Darkly: The Bible, Reflection and Everyday Life* (London: SCM Press, 2016).
Bergsma, J., "The Creation Narratives and the Original Unity of Work and Worship in the Human Vocation", in Loftin, R. K. & Dimsdale, T. (eds), *Work: Theological Foundations and Practical Implications* (London: SCM Press, 2018), pp. 11–29.
Bevans, S. B. & Schroeder, R. P., *Constants in Context: A Theology of Mission for Today* (Maryknoll, NY: Orbis Books, 2004).
Bonhoeffer, D., *Ethics* (London: SCM Press, 1955).
Bonhoeffer, D., *Letters and Papers from Prison (The Enlarged Edition)* (London: SCM Press, 1971).
Book of Common Prayer (1549), <http://justus.anglican.org/resources/bcp/1549/Readings_HolyWeek_1549.htm#Good%20Friday>, accessed 25 September 2020.
Bosch, D. J., *Transforming Mission: Paradigm Shifts in Theology of Mission* (Maryknoll, NY: Orbis Books, 2009 [1991]).
Brueggemann, W., *The Land: Place as Gift, Promise, and Challenge in Biblical Faith* (London: SPCK, 1978).
Brueggemann, W., *The Land: Place as Gift, Promise and Challenge in Biblical Faith* (Minneapolis: Fortress Press, 2002).
Chenu, M. D., *The Theology of Work* (Dublin: Gill and Son, 1963).

Church of England Research and Statistics, *Ministry Statistics 2019*, <https://www.churchofengland.org/sites/default/files/2020-06/Ministry%20Statistics%202019%20report%20FINAL.pdf> (2020), accessed 25 September 2020.

Cosden, D., *A Theology of Work: Work and the New Creation* (Milton Keynes: Paternoster, 2004).

Cosden, D. T., "Work and the New Creation", in Loftin, R. K. & Dimsdale, T. (eds), *Work: Theological Foundations and Practical Implications* (London: SCM Press, 2018), pp. 165–78.

Crites, S., "The Narrative Quality of Experience", in Hauerwas, S. & Jones, L. G. (eds), *Why Narrative? Readings in Narrative Theology* (Grand Rapids, MI: William B Eerdmans Publishing Company, 1989), pp. 65–88.

Crites, S., "The Narrative Quality of Experience", in Graham, E., Walton, H. & Ward, F. (eds), *Theological Reflection: Sources*, (London: SCM Press, 2007), pp. 90–115.

Crockford, S., *Red Rocks and Big Skies: The Sacralisation of Space*, PhD. (London: London School of Economics, 2017).

de Botton, A., *The Pleasures and Sorrows of Work* (London: Hamish Hamilton, 2009).

Edwards, R. & Weller, S., "Shifting Analytic Ontology: Using I-poems in Qualitative Longitudinal Research", *Qualitative Research* 12:2 (2012), pp. 202–17.

Eliade, M., *The Sacred and the Profane: The Nature of Religion* (New York: Harcourt, Brace & World Inc, 1959).

Fiddes, P. S., *Participating in God: A Pastoral Doctrine of the Trinity* (Louisville, KY: Westminster John Knox Press, 2000).

Flett, J. G., "A theology of *missio Dei*", *Theology in Scotland* 21:1 (2014), pp. 69–78.

Foster, P., "Who Wrote 2 Thessalonians? A Fresh Look at an Old Problem", *Journal for the Study of the New Testament* 35:2 (2012), pp. 150–75.

France, R. T., "A pure church? Ecclesiological reflections from the Gospel of Matthew", *Rural Theology* 4:1 (2006), pp. 3–10.

Francis, J. M. M. & Francis, L. J. (eds), *Tentmaking: Perspectives on Self-Supporting Ministry* (Leominster: Gracewing, 1998).

Frei, H. W., *The Eclipse of Biblical Narrative: A Study in Eighteenth and Nineteenth Century Hermeneutics* (New Haven and London: Yale University Press, 1974).

Gage, J., *How shall we sing the Lord's song in a strange land? On being a minister in secular employment*, D Prof. (Cambridge: Anglia Ruskin University, December 2013).

Gage, J., *Being priestly: daring to act for God*, Paper 2, D Prof. (Cambridge: Anglia Ruskin University, July 2014).

Gage, J., *Singing the Lord's song in a strange land: A research proposal for theological reflection on what it means to be a priest in secular employment*, D Prof. (Cambridge: Anglia Ruskin University, June 2015).

Gage, J., "God's gift, not priest-lite cherry-pickers", *Church Times*, 2 March 2018.

Gage, J., letter to the editor in *Church Times*, 21 February 2020.

Ganzevoort, R. R., "Narrative Approaches", in Miller-McLemore, B. J. (ed.), *The Wiley-Blackwell Companion to Practical Theology* (Oxford and Chichester: Wiley-Blackwell, 2012), pp. 214–23.

Ganzevoort, R. R., "Introduction: Religious Stories We Live By", in Ganzevoort, R. R., de Haardt, M. & Scherer-Rath, M. (eds), *Religious Stories We Live By: Narrative Approaches in Theology and Religious Studies* (Leiden: Brill, 2013), pp. 1–17.

Garfield, D., *Neo-Platonic Dualism to Postmodern Fragmentation? A Narrative Inquiry Into Construction and Expression of Self-Identity in Lay Christians in a Contemporary Secular Workplace*, PhD. (Cambridge, UK: Anglia Ruskin University, August 2011).

Giblin, C. H., "The Second Letter to the Thessalonians", in Brown, R. E., Fitzmyer, J. A. & Murphy, R. E. (eds), *The New Jerome Biblical Commentary* (Upper Saddle River, NJ: Prentice-Hall, Inc, 1968), pp. 871–5.

Gilberd, B. C., "Community priests in the New Zealand Anglican church", in Francis, J. M. M. & Francis, L. J. (eds), *Tentmaking: Perspectives on Self-Supporting Ministry* (Leominster: Gracewing, 1998), pp. 127–35.

Graham, E., Walton, H. & Ward, F., *Theological Reflection: Methods* (London: SCM Press, 2005).

Graham, E. L., *Transforming Practice: Pastoral Theology in an Age of Uncertainty* (Eugene, OR: Wipf and Stock Publishers, 2002 [1996]).
Greenwood, R., *Transforming Priesthood: A New Theology of Mission and Ministry* (London: SPCK, 1994).
Hacking, R., *On the Boundary: a vision for non-stipendiary ministry* (Norwich: Canterbury Press, 1990).
Handley Macmath, T., "Interview: Maggie Ross, solitary and theologian", 16 January 2015, <https://www.churchtimes.co.uk/articles/2015/16-january/features/interviews/interview-maggie-ross-solitary-and-theologian>, accessed 25 September 2020.
Hanson, A. T., "Introduction", in *Ministerial Priesthood: Chapters (Preliminary to a study of the Ordinal) on The Rationale of Ministry and the Meaning of Christian Priesthood* (London: SPCK, 1969), pp. i–xxi.
Hauerwas, S., *In Good Company: The Church as Polis* (Notre Dame, IN: University of Notre Dame Press, 1995).
Hauerwas, S. & Wells, S., "The Gift of the Church and the Gifts God Gives It", in Hauerwas, S. & Wells, S. (eds), *The Blackwell Companion to Christian Ethics* (Oxford: Blackwell Publishing, 2004), pp. 13–27.
Hayward, M., *The Sacramental Nature of Priesthood in a Secular Workplace: The MSE as Narrator of the Christian Story*, BA in Theological Studies (Sheffield: University of Sheffield, 2020).
Heer, F. & Hufman, D. A., "The Priest-Workers in France: Origin and backgrounds", *CrossCurrents* 4:3 (1954), pp. 262–74.
Heidegger, M., "An Ontological Consideration of Place", in *The Question of Being* (Albany, NY: NCUP Inc, 1958), pp. 18–26.
Heron, J., *Co-operative Inquiry: Research into the Human Condition* (London: SAGE Publications, 1996).
Heron, J. & Reason, P., "The Practice of Co-operative Inquiry: Research with rather than on People", in Reason, P. & Bradbury, H. (eds), *Handbook of Action Research: Participative Inquiry and Practice* (London: SAGE Publications, 2001), pp. 179–88.

Heron, J. & Reason, P., "Extending Epistemology within a Co-operative Inquiry", in Reason, P. & Bradbury, H. (eds), *Handbook of Action Research: Participative Inquiry and Practice* (London: SAGE Publications, 2008), pp. 366–80.

Hodge, M., *Non-Stipendiary Ministry in the Church of England* (London: General Synod of the Church of England, 1983).

Hopkins, G. M., "As Kingfishers Catch Fire", <https://www.poetryfoundation.org/poems/44389/as-kingfishers-catch-fire>, accessed 25 September 2020.

Hughes, J., *The End of Work: Theological Critiques of Capitalism* (Malden, MA and Oxford: Blackwell, 2007).

Inge, J., *A Christian Theology of Place* (Aldershot: Ashgate, 2003).

Irenaeus, *Against Heresies*, <http://www.newadvent.org/fathers/0103.htm>, accessed 25 September 2020.

Jeanrond, W., *Theological Hermeneutics: Development and Significance* (London: SCM Press, 1991).

John Paul II, *Laborem exercens* (1981), <http://www.vatican.va/holy_father/john_paul_ii/encyclicals/documents/hf_jp-ii_enc_14091981_laborem-exercens_en.html>, accessed 25 September 2020.

John Paul II, *Centesimus annus* (1991), <http://www.vatican.va/holy_father/john_paul_ii/encyclicals/documents/hf_jp-ii_enc_01051991_centesimus-annus_en.html>, accessed 25 September 2020.

Kendzulak, S., *How to Curate an Art Show* (2019), <https://www.thebalancecareers.com/curating-an-art-show-1295610>, accessed 2 December 2020.

King, T. M., *Teilhard's Mass: Approaches to "The Mass on the World"* (New York and Mahwah, NJ: Paulist Press, 2005).

Larive, A., *After Sunday: A Theology of Work* (New York and London: Continuum, 2004).

Leach, J., "Pastoral Theology as Attention", *Contact* 153 (2007), pp. 19–32.

Lees, J., *Self-Supporting Ministry: A Practical Guide* (London: SPCK, 2018).

Loftin, R. K. & Dimsdale, T. (eds), *Work: Theological Foundations and Practical Implications* (London: SCM Press, 2018).
London Institution for Contemporary Christianity, *Your work matters to God*, <https://www.licc.org.uk/about/work/>, accessed 25 September 2020.
Lynch, G., *The Sacred in the Modern World: A Cultural Sociological Approach* (Oxford: Oxford University Press, 2012).
Malbon, E. S., "The Jesus of Mark and the Sea of Galilee", *Journal of Biblical Literature* 103:3 (1984), pp. 363–77.
Mantle, J., *Britain's First Worker-Priests: Radical Ministry in a Post-War Setting* (London: SCM Press, 2000).
Markus, R. A., *Saeculum: History and Society in the Theology of St Augustine* (London: Cambridge University Press, 1970).
McAdams, D. P., *The Stories We Live By: Personal Myths and the Making of the Self* (New York and London: The Guilford Press, 1993).
Mikel Brown, L. & Gilligan, C., *Meeting at the Crossroads: Women's Psychology and Girls' Development* (Cambridge, MA and London: Harvard University Press, 1992).
Moberly, R. C., *Ministerial Priesthood: Chapters (Preliminary to a study of the Ordinal) on The Rationale of Ministry and the Meaning of Christian Priesthood* (London: SPCK, 1969).
Moltmann, J., *Theology of Hope: On the Ground and the Implication of a Christian Eschatology* (London: SCM Press, 2002 [1967]).
Morgan, T., *Self-Supporting Ministry in the Church of England and the Anglican Churches of Wales, Scotland and Ireland* (2011), <http://www.littlemorechurch.org/wp-content/uploads/2012/09/SSM-Report.pdf?LMCL=sOkUod>, accessed 25 September 2020.
Orsi, R. A., *Between Heaven and Earth: The Religious Worlds People Make and the Scholars Who Study Them* (Princeton and Oxford: Princeton University Press, 2005).
Otto, R., *The Idea of the Holy: An inquiry into the non-rational factor in the idea of the divine and its relation to the rational* (Harmondsworth, Middlesex: Penguin Books, 1959 [1917]).

Paul VI, *Lumen gentium* (1964), <http://www.vatican.va/archive/hist_councils/ii_vatican_council/documents/vat-ii_const_19641121_lumen-gentium_en.html>, accessed 25 September 2020.

Pickard, S., *Theological Foundations for Collaborative Ministry* (Farnham, UK: Ashgate, 2009).

Poole, E., "England's cathedrals: magnets for mission", *Church Times*, 14 September 2018, p. 16.

Powell, N., "Euro Disney is hellish workplace, priest reports", *Deseret News*, 29 October 1993, <https://www.deseret.com/1993/10/29/19073619/euro-disney-is-hellish-workplace-priest-reports>, accessed 25 September 2020.

Ramsey, M., *The Christian Priest Today* (London: SPCK, 1985 [1972]).

Ricoeur, P., "From Text to Action: Essays in Hermeneutics, II", in Willows, D. & Swinton, J. (eds), *Spiritual Dimensions of Pastoral Care: Practical Theology in a Multidisciplinary Context* (London: The Athlone Press, 1991), pp. 188–95.

Ross, M., *Pillars of Flame: Power, Priesthood, and Spiritual Maturity* (New York: Seabury Books, 2007 [1988]).

Rossdale, D., "... and he cursed that tree!"—*Views from a Sabbatical* (2010), <https://davidrossdale.wordpress.com/%E2%80%9C%E2%80%A6and-he-cursed-that-tree%E2%80%9D-views-from-a-sabbatical/>, accessed 25 September 2020.

Sayers, D. L., "Why work?", in *Creed or Chaos? and other Essays in popular Theology* (London: Methuen & Co Ltd, 1947), pp. 47–64.

Sheldrake, P., *Spaces for the Sacred: Place, Memory, and Identity* (Baltimore, MD: Johns Hopkins University Press, 2001).

Sheldrake, P., *Befriending Our Desires* (Collegeville, MN: Liturgical Press, 2016).

Sledge, S., *Thin Places* (2014), <http://www.explorefaith.org/mystery/mysteryThinPlaces.html>, accessed 25 September 2020.

Slee, N. & Burns, S. (eds), *Presiding Like a Woman* (London: SPCK, 2010).

St Benedict's Rule for Monasteries (Collegeville, MN: Liturgical Press, 1935).

Stallman, B., *Introduction—Does Leviticus Have Anything to Tell Us about Our Work?* (2017 [2013]), <https://www.theologyofwork.org/old-testament/leviticus-and-work#introduction-does-leviticus-have-anything-to-tell-us-about-our-work>, accessed 25 September 2020.

Stringfellow, W., *An Ethic for Christians and Other Aliens in a Strange Land* (Waco, TX: Word Books, Publisher, 1973).

Taylor, C., *Sources of the Self: The Making of Modern Identity* (Cambridge: Cambridge University Press, 1989).

Taylor, J., "Labour of Love: The Theology of Work in First and Second Thessalonians", in Loftin, R. K. & Dimsdale, T. (eds), *Work: Theological Foundations and Practical Implications* (London: SCM Press, 2018), pp. 49–68.

Theisen, J., *Introduction to the Rule of Saint Benedict* (2015), <https://www.osb.org//gen/rule.html>, accessed 23 September 2020.

Tomlin, G., *The Widening Circle: Priesthood as God's way of blessing the world* (London: SPCK, 2014).

Torry, M., *Bridgebuilders: Workplace Chaplaincy—A History* (Norwich: Canterbury Press, 2010).

Tuan, Y.-F., *Space and Place: The Perspective of Experience* (London: Edward Arnold (Publishers) Ltd, 1977).

Vanier, J., *Drawn into the Mystery of Jesus through the Gospel of John* (London: Darton, Longman and Todd, 2004).

Vatican Council II, *Ad Gentes* (1965), <http://www.vatican.va/archive/hist_councils/ii_vatican_council/documents/vat-ii_decree_19651207_ad-gentes_en.html>, accessed 25 September 2020.

Volf, M., *Work in the Spirit: toward a theology of work* (New York: Oxford University Press, 1991).

von Rad, G., *Genesis: A Commentary* (London: SCM Press Ltd, 1972 [1961]).

Wakeman, H. (ed.), *Circles of Stillness: Thoughts on Contemplative Prayer from the Julian Meetings* (London: Darton, Longman and Todd Ltd, 2002).

Ward, P., "Introduction", in Ward, P. (ed.), *Perspectives on Ecclesiology and Ethnography*, (Grand Rapids, MI/Cambridge, UK: William B Eerdmans Publishing Company, 2012), pp. 1–10.

Wheeler, M., *Martin Heidegger*, Winter 2018, <https://plato.stanford.edu/archives/win2018/entries/heidegger>, accessed 2 December 2020.

Wikipedia Contributors, *Marie-Dominique Chenu* (2020), <https://en.wikipedia.org/wiki/Marie-Dominique_Chenu>, accessed 25 September 2020.

Williams, R., *Faith in the Public Square* (London: Bloomsbury Publishing, 2012).

Williams, R., *Open to Judgement: Sermons and Addresses* (London: Darton, Longman & Todd, 2014).

Williams, R., *On Augustine* (London: Bloomsbury Publishing Plc, 2016).

Williamson, H., "Clocking on: the world of the worker priest", *Church Times*, 6 September 2019.

Witherington, B., *John's Wisdom: A Commentary on the Fourth Gospel* (Cambridge: The Lutterworth Press, 1995).

Witherington, B., *What's in the Word: Rethinking the Socio-Rhetorical Character of the New Testament* (Waco, TX: Baylor University Press, 2009).

Woodhouse, P., *Etty Hillesum: A Life Transformed* (London and New York: Continuum International Publishing Group, 2009).

World Council of Churches, "Baptism, Eucharist and Ministry", Faith and Order Paper No 111 (1982).

World Council of Churches, *Conference on World Mission and Evangelism* (2005), <http://www.mission2005.org/Willingen.559.0.html>, accessed 25 September 2020.

Notes

1. Archbishops' Council, *Common Worship: Ordination Services* (London: Church House Publishing, 2007), p. 17.
2. Archbishops' Council, *Common Worship: Ordination Services*, p. 38.
3. Quoted below with permission.
4. Archbishops' Council, *Common Worship: Ordination Services*, p. 21.
5. Lest you think the parishes were particularly well supplied with priests, only one was a stipendiary parish priest; two were Self-supporting Ministers (SSMs), one full time in ministry (my training incumbent) and the other doing two Sundays a month, and one had a diocesan appointment, keeping his hand in by doing two Sundays a month in our parishes.
6. Ian Adams, *Wilderness Taunts* (Norwich: Canterbury Press, 2016).
7. I was the diocesan officer for SSMs by this stage.
8. Gerhard von Rad, *Genesis: A Commentary* (London: SCM Press Ltd, 1972 [1961]). It was a translation of the original 1961 edition that I was working with at the time.
9. I took the children into Buxton to the east, then drove west either to Keele, where I was doing my PGCE, or to a placement school, then back to Buxton to collect my children, and then home again. During the year, I had moved to Buxton, to simplify things a bit, and in the summer of 1986, we moved again to Belper where I started my teaching career.
10. Florence and the Machine, "Rabbit Heart (Raise It Up)", on the album *Lungs*. It is not at all clear to me now why I was quoting this song, which I am not at all sure I have ever listened to properly. According to that great repository, the internet, the chorus is about ritual sacrifice: <https://genius.com/Florence-the-machine-rabbit-heart-raise-it-up-lyrics>, accessed 29 April 2020.
11. I was writing a book on teaching probability with a colleague.
12. I had been contributing to teaching resources for professional development courses in South Africa, both by going out to teach on residential courses, and by preparing online materials and chapters for printed books.

13 Bishop's Advisory Panel—a forty-eight-hour meeting with three interviewers and other prospective ordinands spread over three days, through which my sponsoring bishop would be given a recommendation as to my suitability to proceed to training for ordained ministry.
14 Hilary Wakeman, (ed.), *Circles of Stillness: Thoughts on Contemplative Prayer from the Julian Meetings* (London: Darton, Longman and Todd Ltd, 2002), pp. 114–15.
15 Not only had I gone through pastoral training in my ministry course, I had been a Samaritan off and on since 1972, and had done a counselling skills course some ten years previously. Training in the specifics of supporting people in such situations was to be provided.
16 My husband continued to work in Milton Keynes when we moved to Ely, leaving early on a Monday morning and returning Friday evening, until he was furloughed and then retired in 2020.
17 Mark Hodge, *Non-Stipendiary Ministry in the Church of England* (London: General Synod of the Church of England, 1983).
18 Dietrich Bonhoeffer, *Letters and Papers from Prison (The Enlarged Edition)* (London: SCM Press, 1971), p. 300.
19 Dietrich Bonhoeffer, *Ethics* (London: SCM Press, 1955), p. 62.
20 Bonhoeffer, *Ethics*, p. 63.
21 Bonhoeffer, *Ethics*, p. 64.
22 William Stringfellow, *An Ethic for Christians and Other Aliens in a Strange Land* (Waco, TX: Word Books, Publisher, 1973), pp. 32–33.
23 R. A. Markus, *Saeculum: History and Society in the Theology of St Augustine* (London: Cambridge University Press, 1970), pp. 17–18.
24 Markus, *Saeculum*, p. 62.
25 Markus, *Saeculum*, p. 55.
26 Rowan Williams, *On Augustine* (London: Bloomsbury Publishing Plc, 2016), loc. 2581.
27 Williams, *On Augustine*, loc. 2581, cf. Augustine, *De civitate Dei*, Book XVIII, 54.
28 Williams, *On Augustine*, loc. 2608–2726.
29 Patrick Woodhouse, *Etty Hillesum: A Life Transformed* (London and New York: Continuum International Publishing Group, 2009), pp. 40–1.
30 Eve Poole, "England's cathedrals: magnets for mission", *Church Times*, 14 September 2018, p. 16.

31 Rudolf Otto, *The Idea of the Holy: An inquiry into the non-rational factor in the idea of the divine and its relation to the rational* (Harmondsworth, Middlesex: Penguin Books, 1959 [1917]).
32 Otto, *The Idea of the Holy*, pp. 39–49.
33 Mircea Eliade, *The Sacred and the Profane: The Nature of Religion* (New York: Harcourt, Brace & World Inc, 1959), p. 11.
34 Eliade, *The Sacred and the Profane*, p. 20.
35 Eliade, *The Sacred and the Profane*, p. 23.
36 Eliade, *The Sacred and the Profane*, p. 96.
37 Gordon Lynch, *The Sacred in the Modern World: A Cultural Sociological Approach* (Oxford: Oxford University Press, 2012), pp. 16–17.
38 Lynch, *The Sacred in the Modern World*, p. 133.
39 Cf. Durkheim, for whom "the sacred is produced by human activities", S. Crockford, *Red Rocks and Big Skies: The Sacralisation of Space* (London: London School of Economics, 2017), p. 106.
40 Robert A. Orsi, *Between Heaven and Earth: The Religious Worlds People Make and the Scholars Who Study Them* (Princeton and Oxford: Princeton University Press, 2005), p. 12.
41 In an article in *The Guardian* on 15 September 2020, Polly Toynbee wrote: "Real life will eventually crash in on Brexit fantasies, but when? How long can people stay in that alternative universe where dreams of sovereignty blot out what's all around them? The religious down the centuries often inhabited dream-worlds of phantom heavens: Brexit voters can hibernate inside their own virtual reality—but not for ever." <https://www.theguardian.com/commentisfree/2020/sep/14/boris-johnson-no-deal-brexit-harm-country-tory-party>, accessed 15 September 2020.
42 Orsi, *Between Heaven and Earth*, pp. 147–8.
43 Cf. Stringfellow, *An Ethic for Christians and Other Aliens in a Strange Land*, pp. 156–7.
44 Pete Ward, "Introduction", in Pete Ward (ed.), *Perspectives on Ecclesiology and Ethnography* (Grand Rapids, MI / Cambridge, UK: William B Eerdmans Publishing Company, 2012), p. 4.
45 Stringfellow, *An Ethic for Christians and Other Aliens in a Strange Land*, p. 76, original italics.
46 Bonhoeffer, *Ethics*, pp. 68–9.

47. Rowan Williams, *Faith in the Public Square* (London: Bloomsbury Publishing, 2012), p. 319.
48. Williams, *Faith in the Public Square*, p. 2.
49. Eliade, *The Sacred and the Profane*, p. 25.
50. Williams, *Faith in the Public Square*, p. 306.
51. David J. Bosch, *Transforming Mission: Paradigm Shifts in Theology of Mission* (Maryknoll, NY: Orbis Books, 2009 [1991]), p. 10.
52. Augustine, *De Trinitate*, V, (2020). Book V.20
53. Bosch, *Transforming Mission*, p. 389.
54. John G. Flett, "A theology of *missio Dei*", *Theology in Scotland* 21:1 (2014), p. 72.
55. Flett, "A theology of *missio Dei*", p. 73.
56. Bosch, *Transforming Mission*, p. 390.
57. The third such; the two previous conferences were held in Edinburgh in 1910, and in Jerusalem in 1928.
58. Bosch, *Transforming Mission*, p. 370.
59. There was a small meeting in Whitby, Canada, in 1947.
60. Bosch, *Transforming Mission*, p. 370.
61. World Council of Churches, *Conference on World Mission and Evangelism*, (2005).
62. Bosch, *Transforming Mission*, p. 373.
63. Bonhoeffer, *Letters and Papers from Prison*, p. 382.
64. Bosch, *Transforming Mission*, p. 371.
65. Paul VI, *Encyclical Letter: Lumen gentium* (1964). section 1.5.
66. Vatican Council II, *Ad Gentes* (1965). Preface.
67. Stephen B. Bevans & Roger P. Schroeder, *Constants in Context: A Theology of Mission for Today* (Maryknoll, NY: Orbis Books, 2004), p. 293; Bosch, *Transforming Mission*, pp. 10, 390.
68. Bosch, *Transforming Mission*, p. 391.
69. Bevans & Schroeder, *Constants in Context*, p. 31.
70. Jürgen Moltmann, *Theology of Hope: On the Ground and the Implication of a Christian Eschatology* (London: SCM Press, 2002 [1967]), p. 312.
71. Bosch, *Transforming Mission*, p. 472.
72. World Council of Churches, "Baptism, Eucharist and Ministry", Faith and Order Paper No 111 (1982).

73 Robin Greenwood, *Transforming Priesthood: A New Theology of Mission and Ministry* (London: SPCK, 1994), p. 142.
74 Bosch, *Transforming Mission*, p. 473.
75 Archbishops' Council, *The Mission and Ministry of the Whole Church: Biblical, Theological and Contemporary Perspectives* (2007). p. iv.
76 *Book of Common Prayer* (1549).
77 Stephen Pickard, *Theological Foundations for Collaborative Ministry* (Farnham, UK: Ashgate, 2009), p. 43.
78 Pickard, *Theological Foundations for Collaborative Ministry*, p. 41.
79 Bosch, *Transforming Mission*, p. 381.
80 Bosch, *Transforming Mission*, pp. 386–7.
81 Werner Jeanrond, *Theological Hermeneutics: Development and Significance* (London: SCM Press, 1991), p. 172.
82 M. Hodge, *Non-Stipendiary Ministry in the Church of England* (London: General Synod of the Church of England, 1983), p. 21.
83 Hodge, *Non-Stipendiary Ministry in the Church of England*, p. 9, as given in The Pluralities Act of 1838, which was based on a Statute of 1529.
84 The ordination of women in the Anglican communion dates from the 1970s, although the first woman to be ordained priest was Florence Li Tim-Oi on 25 January 1944, during the crisis caused by the Japanese invasion of Hong Kong. After the war, she resigned her licence, while remaining in priestly orders, <https://www.anglican.ca/faith/worship/resources/li-tim-oi/>, accessed 20 November 2020. Ordination of women as priests in the C of E dates from 1994, <https://www.independent.co.uk/news/send-down-your-holy-spirit-upon-your-servant-angela-history-is-made-as-the-church-of-england-ordains-1428835.html>, accessed 20 November 2020.
85 Roland Allen, *Missionary Methods: St Paul's or Ours?* (Grand Rapids, MI: Wm B Eerdmans Publishing Co, 1962).
86 Hodge, *Non-Stipendiary Ministry in the Church of England*, p. 11.
87 Hodge, *Non-Stipendiary Ministry in the Church of England*, p. 21. Bishop Ronald Hall began ordaining NSMs in Hong Kong in the late 1930s; it was he who subsequently ordained Florence Li Tim-Oi, <http://www.hkskh.org/content.aspx?id=12&lang=1>, accessed 28 September 2020.
88 Hodge, *Non-Stipendiary Ministry in the Church of England*, p. 12.
89 Hodge, *Non-Stipendiary Ministry in the Church of England*, pp. 13–14.

90 Convocation of Canterbury Report No 638: Report of the Joint Committee on the Proposed Draft Canon 83 (and 81), pp. 14–15, cited in Hodge, *Non-Stipendiary Ministry in the Church of England*, p. 14.

91 Archbishops' Council, *Canons of the Church of England*, (2019).

92 For those of us who are not paid a stipend, permission to earn our living in some manner is now assumed without question.

93 Cf. D. Garfield, *Neo-Platonic Dualism to Postmodern Fragmentation? A Narrative Inquiry Into Construction and Expression of Self-Identity in Lay Christians in a Contemporary Secular Workplace* (Cambridge, UK: Anglia Ruskin University, August 2011).

94 Rod Hacking, *On the Boundary: a vision for non-stipendiary ministry* (Norwich: Canterbury Press, 1990), p. vii. Carey was then Bishop of Bath and Wells, later Archbishop of Canterbury.

95 Hacking, *On the Boundary*, pp. 23–4.

96 Teresa Morgan, *Self-Supporting Ministry in the Church of England and the Anglican Churches of Wales, Scotland and Ireland*, (2011), p. 5.

97 Hodge, *Non-Stipendiary Ministry in the Church of England*, p. 86.

98 Morgan, *Self-Supporting Ministry in the Church of England and the Anglican Churches of Wales, Scotland and Ireland*, p. 12.

99 Currently at 27.2 per cent, 2019 figures. Church of England Research and Statistics, *Ministry Statistics 2019*, (2020).

100 Hacking, *On the Boundary*, p. 26.

101 The event has not been entirely erased from the internet, however, since the text of Bishop Steven Croft's sermon on that occasion is still available: <http://www.with-intent.confiteor.org.uk/steven-croft-southwark-ordination-cours-anniversary.html>, accessed 5 December 2018. The Church of England website has undergone major changes in the past few years, so I assume that the page linking this report was among those removed because they did not fit into the new structure.

102 Michael Ramsey, *The Christian Priest Today* (London: SPCK, 1985 [1972]), p. 7.

103 R. C. Moberly, *Ministerial Priesthood: Chapters (Preliminary to a study of the Ordinal) on The Rationale of Ministry and the Meaning of Christian Priesthood* (London: SPCK, 1969); cf. Greenwood, *Transforming Priesthood*; Pickard, *Theological Foundations for Collaborative Ministry*.

104 A. T. Hanson, "Introduction", in (ed.), *Ministerial Priesthood: Chapters (Preliminary to a study of the Ordinal) on The Rationale of Ministry and the Meaning of Christian Priesthood*, (London: SPCK, 1969), p. viii; cf. Pickard, *Theological Foundations for Collaborative Ministry*.
105 Greenwood, *Transforming Priesthood*, p. 8.
106 Hanson, "Introduction", pp. i–xxi.
107 Greenwood, *Transforming Priesthood*, p. 78; Pickard, *Theological Foundations for Collaborative Ministry*.
108 Pickard, *Theological Foundations for Collaborative Ministry*, p. 39.
109 Greenwood, *Transforming Priesthood*, p. 30.
110 Nicola Slee & Stephen Burns (eds), *Presiding Like a Woman* (London: SPCK, 2010).
111 Greenwood, *Transforming Priesthood*; cf. Pickard, *Theological Foundations for Collaborative Ministry*, pp. 36–8.
112 E.g. Friedrich Heer & Dorothy A. Hufman, "The Priest-Workers in France: Origin and backgrounds", *CrossCurrents* 4:3 (1954), pp. 262–74; John Mantle, *Britain's First Worker-Priests: Radical Ministry in a Post-War Setting* (London: SCM Press, 2000), p. 1.
113 Malcolm Torry, *Bridgebuilders: Workplace Chaplaincy—A History* (Norwich: Canterbury Press, 2010), p. 71; cf. Heer & Hufman, "The Priest-Workers in France: Origin and backgrounds".
114 E.g. Torry, *Bridgebuilders*, p. 71.
115 Heer & Hufman, "The Priest-Workers in France: Origin and backgrounds", p. 270–1; cf. Torry, *Bridgebuilders*, p. 72.
116 Torry, *Bridgebuilders*, pp. ix, 30.
117 Torry, *Bridgebuilders*, p. 72.
118 Torry, *Bridgebuilders*, p. 59.
119 Torry, *Bridgebuilders*, p. 60.
120 Torry, *Bridgebuilders*, pp. 64–5.
121 Torry, *Bridgebuilders*, p. 64.
122 Torry, *Bridgebuilders*, p. 73.
123 Mantle, *Britain's First Worker-Priests*, p. 128.
124 Torry, *Bridgebuilders*, p. 74; James M. M. Francis & Leslie J. Francis (eds), *Tentmaking: Perspectives on Self-Supporting Ministry* (Leominster: Gracewing, 1998), p. 299.
125 Mantle, *Britain's First Worker-Priests*, p. 135.

126 Hodge, *Non-Stipendiary Ministry in the Church of England*.
127 Hodge, *Non-Stipendiary Ministry in the Church of England*, p. 86.
128 Francis & Francis (eds), *Tentmaking*, p. 91.
129 Bishop of Madurai Diocese, 1947–59.
130 Francis & Francis (eds), *Tentmaking*, p. 107.
131 Bruce C. Gilberd, "Community priests in the New Zealand Anglican church", in Francis, & Francis (eds), *Tentmaking*, p. 131.
132 Mantle, *Britain's First Worker-Priests*, p. 273.
133 Mantle, *Britain's First Worker-Priests*, p. 273.
134 Hodge, *Non-Stipendiary Ministry in the Church of England*, pp. 62–8.
135 Paul S. Fiddes, *Participating in God: A Pastoral Doctrine of the Trinity* (Louisville, KY: Westminster, John Knox Press, 2000), p. 77.
136 Fiddes, *Participating in God*, p. 74.
137 Fiddes, *Participating in God*, pp. 78–9.
138 Fiddes, *Participating in God*, p. 281.
139 Fiddes, *Participating in God*, p. 294.
140 Cf. David Rossdale, "... *and he cursed that tree!"—Views from a Sabbatical*, (2010).
141 Fiddes, *Participating in God*, p. 215.
142 Christians in Secular Ministry, <http://www.chrism.org.uk/>, accessed 27 April 2020.
143 Jenny Gage, *Church Times*, 21 February 2020.
144 Rowan Williams, *Open to Judgement: Sermons and Addresses* (London: Darton, Longman & Todd, 2014).
145 Jenny Gage, *Church Times*, 21 February 2020.
146 Church of England Research and Statistics, *Ministry Statistics 2019*, (2020).
147 The blanket term for all who are licensed and ordained deacons and priests is self-supporting minister (SSM). OLMs are ordained local ministers, who are restricted to the diocese or context in which they were ordained, and who cannot automatically move elsewhere and have their status recognized. NSMs are then those SSMs whose status is nationally recognized.
148 John Heron, *Co-operative Inquiry: Research into the Human Condition* (London: SAGE Publications, 1996); John Heron & Peter Reason, "The Practice of Co-operative Inquiry: Research with rather than on People", in P. Reason & H. Bradbury (eds), *Handbook of Action Research: Participative Inquiry and Practice* (London: SAGE Publications, 2001), pp. 179–88; John

Heron & Peter Reason, "Extending Epistemology within a Co-operative Inquiry", in Reason & Bradbury (eds), *Handbook of Action Research*, pp. 366–80.

149 Lyn Mikel Brown & Carol Gilligan, *Meeting at the Crossroads: Women's Psychology and Girls' Development* (Cambridge, MA and London: Harvard University Press, 1992); Rosalind Edwards & Susie Weller, "Shifting Analytic Ontology: Using I-poems in Qualitative Longitudinal Research", *Qualitative Research* 12:2 (2012), pp. 202–17.

150 I think this is actually shared by the diocesan bishop with the incumbent, and so was not perhaps entirely appropriate, but in a way, that made it even more moving to be included in the cure of souls in our parishes.

151 Jonny Baker, see <https://jonnybaker.blogs.com/jonnybaker/>, accessed 2 December 2020.

152 Jonny Baker, *Curating Worship* (London: SPCK, 2010), pp. 4–13.

153 Susan Kendzulak, *How to Curate an Art Show* (2019) at <https://www.thebalancecareers.com/curating-an-art-show-1295610>, accessed 2 December 2020.

154 Jane Leach, "Pastoral Theology as Attention", *Contact* 153 (2007), pp. 22–3.

155 Elaine Graham, Heather Walton & Frances Ward, *Theological Reflection: Methods* (London: SCM Press, 2005), pp. 78–108.

156 Graham, Walton & Ward, *Theological Reflection: Methods*, p. 95.

157 Graham, Walton & Ward, *Theological Reflection: Methods*, p. 78.

158 Graham, Walton & Ward, *Theological Reflection: Methods*, p. 79.

159 Hans W. Frei, *The Eclipse of Biblical Narrative: A Study in Eighteenth and Nineteenth Century Hermeneutics* (New Haven and London: Yale University Press, 1974), p. 280.

160 Graham, Walton & Ward, *Theological Reflection: Methods*, p. 96.

161 Ben Witherington, *What's in the Word: Rethinking the Socio-Rhetorical Character of the New Testament* (Waco, TX: Baylor University Press, 2009), p. 2.

162 Ben Witherington, *John's Wisdom: A Commentary on the Fourth Gospel* (Cambridge: The Lutterworth Press, 1995), p. 22.

163 Augustine, *Confessions* (Harmondsworth: Penguin Books Ltd, 1961), p. 21.

164 Dan P. McAdams, *The Stories We Live By: Personal Myths and the Making of the Self* (New York and London: The Guilford Press, 1993), p. 11, original italics; cf. Herbert Anderson & Edward Foley, "The Power of Storytelling", in

Elaine Graham, Heather Walton & Frances Ward (eds), *Theological Reflection: Sources* (London: SCM Press, 2007), pp. 127–38.

165 Jenny Gage, *How shall we sing the Lord's song in a strange land? On being a minister in secular employment* (Cambridge: Anglia Ruskin University, December 2013), p. iii.

166 Jenny Gage, *Being priestly: daring to act for God* (Cambridge: Anglia Ruskin University, July 2014).

167 Jenny Gage, *Singing the Lord's song in a strange land: A research proposal for theological reflection on what it means to be a priest in secular employment* (Cambridge: Anglia Ruskin University, June 2015), p. iii.

168 Paul VI, *Encyclical Letter: Lumen gentium* (1964). II.10.

169 Baptist Union of Great Britain, *In honour of Paul Fiddes* (2014). Paul Fiddes was Professor of Systematic Theology at the University of Oxford from 2002.

170 Fiddes, *Participating in God*.

171 World Council of Churches, "Baptism, Eucharist and Ministry", Faith and Order Paper No 111 (1982), p. 18.

172 Archbishops' Council, *Canons of the Church of England*, (2019). Canon B12.

173 Cf. World Council of Churches, "Baptism, Eucharist and Ministry".

174 Hodge, *Non-Stipendiary Ministry in the Church of England*.

175 Bonhoeffer, *Letters and Papers from Prison*, pp. 369–70.

176 Bonhoeffer, *Letters and Papers from Prison*, p. 5; cf. "where Christians, in the same frailty and tension as any other human beings, become participants in specific violence they do so confessionally, acknowledging throughout the sin of it". Stringfellow, *An Ethic for Christians and Other Aliens in a Strange Land*, pp. 132–3.

177 This echoes what an MSE is quoted as saying in John Lees, *Self-Supporting Ministry: A Practical Guide* (London: SPCK, 2018), p. 39, that MSEs rarely engage in direct evangelism, but are "getting on with the job and doing it as well as you can while working alongside and supporting other people".

178 He compared this exchange to the Monty Python sketch "The 4 Yorkshiremen", <http://www.montypython.net/scripts/4york.php>, accessed 20 November 2020.

179 Charles Taylor, *Sources of the Self: The Making of Modern Identity* (Cambridge: Cambridge University Press, 1989), p. 35.

180 Graham, Walton & Ward, *Theological Reflection: Methods*, pp. 18, 20.

[181] Cf. Stephen Crites, "The Narrative Quality of Experience", in Graham, Walton & Ward (eds), *Theological Reflection: Sources*, pp. 90–115; also published in Stanley Hauerwas & L. Gregory Jones (eds), *Why Narrative? Readings in Narrative Theology* (Grand Rapids, MI: William B Eerdmans Publishing Company, 1989), pp. 65–88.

[182] R. Ruard Ganzevoort, "Introduction: Religious Stories We Live By", in R. Ruard Ganzevoort, Maaike de Haardt & Michael Scherer-Rath (eds), *Religious Stories We Live By: Narrative Approaches in Theology and Religious Studies* (Leiden: Brill, 2013), pp. 1–17.

[183] Crites, "The Narrative Quality of Experience", in Hauerwas & Jones (eds), *Why Narrative?*, pp. 66, 70.

[184] Crites, "The Narrative Quality of Experience", in Hauerwas & Jones (eds), *Why Narrative?*, p. 71.

[185] R. Ruard Ganzevoort, "Narrative Approaches", in Bonnie J. Miller-McLemore (ed.), *The Wiley-Blackwell Companion to Practical Theology* (Oxford and Chichester: Wiley-Blackwell, 2012), p. 216.

[186] Ganzevoort, "Introduction: Religious Stories We Live By", in Ganzevoort, de Haardt & Scherer-Rath (eds), *Religious Stories We Live By*, pp. 2–3; cf. Crites, "The Narrative Quality of Experience", in Hauerwas & Jones (eds), *Why Narrative?*, pp. 65–88.

[187] Ganzevoort, "Narrative Approaches", pp. 214–23.

[188] Cf. Crites, "The Narrative Quality of Experience", in Hauerwas & Jones (eds), *Why Narrative?*

[189] Cf. Paul Ricoeur, "From Text to Action: Essays in Hermeneutics, II", in David Willows & John Swinton (eds), *Spiritual Dimensions of Pastoral Care: Practical Theology in a Multidisciplinary Context* (London: The Athlone Press, 1991), pp. 188–95.

[190] Elaine L. Graham, *Transforming Practice: Pastoral Theology in an Age of Uncertainty* (Eugene, OR: Wipf and Stock Publishers, 2002 [1996]), pp. 30, 107.

[191] Kwame Anthony Appiah, *The Ethics of Identity* (Princeton, NJ: Princeton University Press, 2005), pp. 17–18.

[192] Kwame Anthony Appiah, "Identity, Authenticity, Survival: Multicultural Societies and Social Reproduction", in Amy Gutmann (ed.), *Multiculturalism: Examining the Politics of Recognition* (Princeton and Chichester: Princeton University Press, 1994), p. 151.

[193] Appiah, *The Ethics of Identity*, p. 22.
[194] Appiah, *The Ethics of Identity*, pp. 65–70.
[195] Appiah, *The Ethics of Identity*, p. 106.
[196] Maggie Ross, *Pillars of Flame: Power, Priesthood, and Spiritual Maturity* (New York: Seabury Books, 2007 [1988]), p. xxvii.
[197] Ross, *Pillars of Flame*, p. xxxiii.
[198] In an interview for the *Church Times*, Ross commented on "the spiritual suicide of ordination". Terence Handley Macmath, *Interview: Maggie Ross, solitary and theologian*, 16 January 2015.
[199] Ross, *Pillars of Flame*, p. 19.
[200] Ross, *Pillars of Flame*, p. 28, original italics.
[201] He had composed a setting of the *Common Worship* text of the Eucharist for the occasion, which was sung by members of the choirs of the churches in the benefice, and the choir I sang with, whose director led the music—a most amazing ordination gift from everyone concerned!
[202] Graham Tomlin, *The Widening Circle: Priesthood as God's way of blessing the world* (London: SPCK, 2014), p. ix.
[203] John Lees, *Self-Supporting Ministry: A Practical Guide* (London: SPCK, 2018), p. 47.
[204] Moberly, *Ministerial Priesthood*, p. 92.
[205] Moberly, *Ministerial Priesthood*, p. 68.
[206] Cf. Appiah, *The Ethics of Identity*, p. 20—our identity is fashioned through our interactions with others.
[207] Archbishops' Council, *No ordinary ministry: Ministers in secular employment*, n.d.
[208] For instance, Head of Department.
[209] Appiah, *The Ethics of Identity*, pp. 21–2.
[210] Appiah, *The Ethics of Identity*, p. 24.
[211] My own attempt, post-ordination, to run three lunchtime sessions on the relationship between faith and work was similarly unsuccessful: one person came late to the middle session; otherwise I was on my own apart from the presence at the first two sessions of the university chaplain to staff.
[212] Hodge, *Non-Stipendiary Ministry in the Church of England*, p. 53.
[213] Hodge, *Non-Stipendiary Ministry in the Church of England*, pp. 42–3.
[214] Hodge, *Non-Stipendiary Ministry in the Church of England*, p. 43.

215 Cf. Morgan, *Self-Supporting Ministry in the Church of England and the Anglican Churches of Wales, Scotland and Ireland*; Lees, *Self-Supporting Ministry*, p. 16.
216 Lees, *Self-Supporting Ministry*, p. 40.
217 Appiah, *The Ethics of Identity*, p. 64.
218 Augustine, *Confessions*, p. 21.
219 Philip Sheldrake, *Befriending Our Desires* (Collegeville, MN: Liturgical Press, 2016), p. xi.
220 Sheldrake, *Befriending Our Desires*, p. xi.
221 Dorothy L. Sayers, "Why work?", in *Creed or Chaos? and other Essays in popular Theology*, pp. 54–5.
222 Alain de Botton, *The Pleasures and Sorrows of Work* (London: Hamish Hamilton, 2009), p. 30.
223 E.g. Miroslav Volf, *Work in the Spirit: toward a theology of work* (New York: Oxford University Press, 1991); Darrell Cosden, *A Theology of Work: Work and the New Creation* (Milton Keynes: Paternoster, 2004); Armand Larive, *After Sunday: A Theology of Work* (New York and London: Continuum, 2004); John Hughes, *The End of Work: Theological Critiques of Capitalism* (Malden, MA and Oxford: Blackwell, 2007); R. Keith Loftin & Trey Dimsdale (eds), *Work: Theological Foundations and Practical Implications* (London: SCM Press, 2018).
224 Cf. Larive, *After Sunday*, p. 155.
225 Cf. Volf, *Work in the Spirit*; Larive, *After Sunday*.
226 John Bergsma, "The Creation Narratives and the Original Unity of Work and Worship in the Human Vocation", in Loftin & Dimsdale (eds), *Work*, pp. 12–13.
227 Cf. Bob Stallman, *Introduction—Does Leviticus Have Anything to Tell Us about Our Work?*, (2017 [2013]), at <https://www.theologyofwork.org/old-testament/leviticus-and-work/introduction-does-leviticus-have-anything-to-tell-us-about-our-work>, accessed 2 December 2020.
228 John Taylor, "Labour of Love: The Theology of Work in First and Second Thessalonians", in Loftin & Dimsdale (eds), *Work*, p. 49.
229 E.g. Paul Foster, "Who Wrote 2 Thessalonians? A Fresh Look at an Old Problem", *Journal for the Study of the New Testament* 35:2 (2012), p. 150; Charles Homer Giblin, "The Second Letter to the Thessalonians", in Raymond E. Brown, Joseph A. Fitzmyer & Roland E. Murphy (eds), *The New Jerome*

Biblical Commentary (Upper Saddle River, NJ: Prentice-Hall, Inc, 1968), p. 871.

[230] The attribution of the Rule to St Benedict is "relatively certain", but its date cannot be given more precisely than 530–560. Jerome Theisen, *Introduction to the Rule of Saint Benedict* (2015).

[231] *St Benedict's Rule for Monasteries* (Collegeville, MN: Liturgical Press, 1935), pp. 68–9.

[232] Aquinas, Thomas, *Summa Theologiae*, II-II, Q.187.A3.

[233] Aquinas, Thomas, *Summa Theologiae*, II-II, Q.182.A3,4.

[234] Larive, *After Sunday*, p. 25.

[235] Volf, *Work in the Spirit*, p. 106.

[236] Archbishops' Council, *No ordinary ministry: Ministers in secular employment*.

[237] London Institution for Contemporary Christianity, *Your work matters to God*, n.d.

[238] Sayers, "Why work?", p. 47.

[239] John Paul II, *Laborem exercens* (1981), para 3, original italics.

[240] Hughes, *The End of Work*, p. 12.

[241] Cf. Stanley Hauerwas, *In Good Company: The Church as Polis* (Notre Dame, IN: University of Notre Dame Press, 1995).

[242] He is also credited with "being the grandfather of the liberation theology movement". Wikipedia Contributors, *Marie-Dominique Chenu*, (2020).

[243] M. D. Chenu, *The Theology of Work* (Dublin: Gill and Son, 1963), p. 3.

[244] Chenu, *The Theology of Work*, p. 6.

[245] Chenu, *The Theology of Work*, p. 10.

[246] Chenu, *The Theology of Work*, p. 22.

[247] Chenu, *The Theology of Work*, p. 22.

[248] Chenu, *The Theology of Work*, p. 5.

[249] John Paul II, *Laborem exercens* (1981); cf. John Paul II, *Centesimus annus* (1991), para 31.

[250] Cf. Hughes, *The End of Work*, p. 17.

[251] Hughes, *The End of Work*, p. 17.

[252] John Paul II, *Laborem exercens* (1981), para 27.

[253] Hauerwas, *In Good Company*, p. 109.

[254] Volf, *Work in the Spirit*, p. 7.

[255] Volf, *Work in the Spirit*, p. 25.

[256] Volf, *Work in the Spirit*, pp. 36–42.

257 Volf, *Work in the Spirit*, pp. 43–5.
258 Volf, *Work in the Spirit*, p. 77.
259 Cf. Moltmann, *Theology of Hope*, p. 79.
260 Volf, *Work in the Spirit*, pp. 89–92; John Paul II, *Laborem exercens* (1981), para 25.
261 Irenaeus, *Against Heresies*, V.36.1.
262 Volf, *Work in the Spirit*, p. 100.
263 Volf, *Work in the Spirit*, pp. 101–2.
264 Volf, *Work in the Spirit*, pp. 111–14.
265 Volf, *Work in the Spirit*, p. 118; cf. Revelation 21:24–6.
266 Cf. Volf, *Work in the Spirit*, p. 91; Darrell Cosden, "Work and the New Creation", in Loftin & Dimsdale (eds), *Work*, p. 171.
267 John Paul II, *Laborem exercens* (1981), 9.
268 Irenaeus, *Against Heresies*, IV.38.3.
269 Cosden, "Work and the New Creation", p. 172.
270 Irenaeus, *Against Heresies*, V.16.2.
271 Cf. Cosden, "Work and the New Creation", p. 167; Hauerwas, *In Good Company*.
272 John Paul II, *Laborem exercens* (1981), para 9, original italics.
273 Cf. Chenu, *The Theology of Work*, p. 5.
274 Hughes, *The End of Work*, p. 219.
275 Larive, *After Sunday*, pp. 149–55.
276 D. Garfield, *Neo-Platonic Dualism to Postmodern Fragmentation? A Narrative Inquiry Into Construction and Expression of Self-Identity in Lay Christians in a Contemporary Secular Workplace* (Cambridge: Anglia Ruskin University, August 2011); cf. Chapter 1.
277 Archbishops' Council, *Setting God's People Free* (GS 2056) (2017).
278 Lees, *Self-Supporting Ministry*, p. 39.
279 Woodhouse, *Etty Hillesum: A Life Transformed*.
280 Eve Poole, "England's cathedrals: magnets for mission", *Church Times*, 14 September 2018, p. 16.
281 Lees, *Self-Supporting Ministry*, pp. 48, 58.
282 Sayers, "Why work?", p. 47.
283 John Paul II, *Laborem exercens* (1981), para 3, original italics.
284 Her husband is also a priest, and at the time, they were licensed to the same parish.

285 Stringfellow, *An Ethic for Christians and Other Aliens in a Strange Land*, p. 129.
286 Gage, *How shall we sing the Lord's song in a strange land? On being a minister in secular employment*.
287 Although I struggle with the violence of the final verses, with the reference to dashing babies against the rock, understanding Babylon as the place of violence and death provides a frame of reference in which it can be understood.
288 Zoe Bennett & Christopher Rowland, *In a Glass Darkly: The Bible, Reflection and Everyday Life* (London: SCM Press, 2016), p. 96.
289 If my eldest daughter, then aged nearly six, was to go to school, she needed the precise immunization schedule required in Arizona. Part of the cultural adjustment I had yet to make was realizing that having health insurance meant that I could simply have taken her to see a pediatrician, rather than waiting in line for the free, public clinic.
290 Written by Dewey Bunnell, recorded by the band America in 1971.
291 "'Do not fear, for I have redeemed you; I have called you by name, you are mine. . . . everyone who is called by my name, whom I created for my glory, whom I formed and made.'" (Isaiah 43:1–7)
292 Charles Taylor, *Sources of the Self*, p. 28.
293 Taylor, *Sources of the Self*, pp. 29–30.
294 John Inge, *A Christian Theology of Place* (Aldershot: Ashgate, 2003), p. 2.
295 Yi-Fu Tuan, *Space and Place: The Perspective of Experience* (London: Edward Arnold (Publishers) Ltd, 1977), p. 73.
296 Michael Wheeler, "Martin Heidegger", <https://plato.stanford.edu/entries/heidegger/>, accessed 2 December 2020.
297 Inge, *A Christian Theology of Place*, p. 18.
298 Martin Heidegger, "An Ontological Consideration of Place", in *The Question of Being* (Albany, NY: NCUP Inc, 1958), p. 101.
299 Walter Brueggemann, *The Land: Place as Gift, Promise, and Challenge in Biblical Faith* (London: SPCK, 1978), pp. 10–13.
300 Inge, *A Christian Theology of Place*, p. 56.
301 Cf. Inge, *A Christian Theology of Place*, p. 12.
302 A digital service tax came into effect in the UK in 2020, part of attempts to hold global companies accountable in the country where their profits

are made: <https://www.computing.co.uk/news/4019604/google-amazon-digital-service-tax>, accessed 25 September 2020.
303 Eliade, *The Sacred and the Profane*.
304 E.g. Sharlande Sledge, *Thin Places*, (2014).
305 Inge, *A Christian Theology of Place*, pp. 78–9.
306 In Genesis 1, "the earth was a formless void" prior to God's creative action of sending a wind "over the face of the waters". Images of sea monsters were common on early maps, indicating "there's bad stuff out there", but apparently the phrase "here be dragons" is only found on two globes, both dating from the early sixteenth century. Roman and mediaeval cartographers used *hic sunt leones* for unknown territories. <https://en.wikipedia.org/wiki/Here_be_dragons>, accessed 25 September 2020.
307 Eliade, *The Sacred and the Profane*, pp. 31–2.
308 Philip Sheldrake, *Spaces for the Sacred: Place, Memory, and Identity* (Baltimore, MD: Johns Hopkins University Press, 2001), p. 5.
309 E.g. <https://blacklivesmatter.com>, accessed 25 September 2020.
310 Crockford, *Red Rocks and Big Skies*, pp. 90–1.
311 Sheldrake, *Spaces for the Sacred*, p. 30.
312 Sheldrake, *Spaces for the Sacred*, p. 38.
313 E. S. Malbon, "The Jesus of Mark and the Sea of Galilee", *Journal of Biblical Literature* 103:3 (1984), p. 363.
314 Malbon, "The Jesus of Mark and the Sea of Galilee", p. 375.
315 Markus, *Saeculum*, p. 23.
316 Markus, *Saeculum*, p. 173.
317 Cf. Bonhoeffer, *Ethics*; also Richard T. France, "A pure church? Ecclesiological reflections from the Gospel of Matthew", *Rural Theology* 4:1 (2006), who argued that this is a matter of ecclesiology, and that rural village churches in particular cannot be communities of the saved only.
318 Archbishops' Council, *Setting God's People Free* (GS 2056), (2017), p. 15.
319 Archbishops' Council, *Setting God's People Free* (GS 2056), (2017), p. 2.
320 This remark followed a story about someone who had ministered among dockers in Britain, who had observed that black dockers would have loaded the ship, while white dockers unloaded it, with neither group knowing or caring about the lives of the other, but being inter-connected nevertheless.
321 Lees, *Self-Supporting Ministry*, p. 56.

[322] Nicholas Powell, "Euro Disney is hellish workplace, priest reports", *Deseret News*, 29 October 1993.
[323] Brueggemann, *The Land*, pp. 199–200.
[324] Woodhouse, *Etty Hillesum*, pp. 40–1.
[325] Cf. Bonhoeffer, *Ethics*, p. 68.
[326] M. Hayward, *The Sacramental Nature of Priesthood in a Secular Workplace: The MSE as Narrator of the Christian Story* (Sheffield: University of Sheffield, 2020).
[327] Jean Vanier, *Drawn into the Mystery of Jesus through the Gospel of John* (London: Darton, Longman and Todd, 2004), p. 267.
[328] Fiddes, *Participating in God*, p. 215.
[329] Cf. Stanley Hauerwas & Samuel Wells, "The Gift of the Church and the Gifts God Gives It", in Stanley Hauerwas & Samuel Wells (eds), *The Blackwell Companion to Christian Ethics* (Oxford: Blackwell Publishing, 2004), pp. 13–27.
[330] Hauerwas & Wells, "The Gift of the Church and the Gifts God Gives It", p. 19.
[331] Francis & Francis (eds), *Tentmaking*, p. 2.
[332] Jenny Gage, "God's gift, not priest-lite cherry-pickers", *Church Times*, 2 March 2018.
[333] Hugh Williamson, "Clocking on: the world of the worker priest", *Church Times*, 6 September 2019.
[334] Teilhard de Chardin's Mass on the World, in Thomas M. King, *Teilhard's Mass: Approaches to "The Mass on the World"* (New York and Mahwah, NJ: Paulist Press, 2005), p. 145. He wrote at least two versions of this section, in 1918 and again in 1923.
[335] Gerard Manley Hopkins, "As Kingfishers Catch Fire".

EU GPSR Authorized Representative:

LOGOS EUROPE, 9 rue Nicolas Poussin, 17000 La Rochelle, France

contact@logoseurope.eu